Mediation
Empowerment in Conflict Management

Kathy Domenici
The University of New Mexico

WAVELAND
PRESS, INC.
Prospect Heights, Illinois

For information about this book, write or call:

Waveland Press, Inc.
P.O. Box 400
Prospect Heights, Illinois 60070
(847) 634-0081

Contents

Preface

This textbook covers a wide range of conflict management opportunities. It is particularly directed to students of mediation—those individuals interested in receiving the skills training necessary to be certified as mediators. Mediation is a component of the rapidly growing ADR field (Alternative Dispute Resolution). Mediators can apply this training to numerous disciplines, including: communication, psychology, law, political science, sociology, social work, anthropology, and architecture. The work of a mediator extends beyond assisting individuals with specific disputes; it can educate them on the use of constructive conflict management as a means to a more effective, efficient, and healthy human environment.

A special note of thanks goes to the Communication and Journalism Department at the University of New Mexico, which supported my belief that much conflict stems from ineffective communication. Encouragement and training was given by a local mediation organization, The Mediation Alliance, and by The University of New Mexico Mediation Clinic. A solid base for this project was provided by my cohorts at the Hewlett Institute for Socio-Legal Dispute Resolution at The Ohio State University in June 1993. Three of the mediators from the University of New Mexico have shared entries from their conflict journals. In the sections marked "journal entry," words from Jeff Grant, Allison Frank, and Robert Sher are offered for a broader perspective. To the numerous scholars and practitioners dedicated to peaceful conflict management, I offer this book as a part of our joint effort.

Introduction

Discussions of mediation and other forms of dispute resolution often revolve around the use, misuse, and manipulation of power. When a situation exists with both conflict *and* an imbalance of power, managing the situation effectively requires attention to the power issue. Typically, power imbalances are evidenced by who has the most money; who is the boss and who is the subordinate; who is better educated and more experienced. More subtle power imbalances occur because of individual differences. Sometimes the less empowered individual is the one without the communication skills needed in the situation. Other times, the person with the not-as-common skin color, age, religion, or last name experiences a lesser degree of power. The mediator must manage these power imbalances. The exploration of "mediation" in this book makes power issues a focal point in identifying and understanding the process. Before beginning the exploration of mediation, let's take a brief look at power.

Donohue and Kolt (1992) believe that to understand power one needs to understand how people manipulate dependencies. According to the Principle of Least Interest, the person with the least interest or investment in a relationship has the most power because that person has less at risk and, if so inclined, can take advantage of the fact that the other party has

more to lose. In a conflict situation, the least
empowered party depends on the powerful party for
many decisions and opportunities. For example, in a
conflict between a boss and a subordinate, the subordinate depends on the boss for the job, wages,
advancement, and self-esteem. Power is a relational concept. According to
Donohue and Kolt (1992),

> Power really comes down to a dependency
> issue. The more people try to control one
> another, the more they confirm their
> interdependency. A couple that is very
> much in love controls each other's lives.
> People that love their leaders depend on
> those leaders for guidance. Love and
> dependency give those leaders tremendous
> control over their followers. (p. 91)

Because mediation is an impartial process, the
message is conveyed that the parties are viewed
equally. They are greeted, seated, listened to, and
responded to in similar respectful ways. The process
is a nonjudgmental forum where relational dependencies can be minimized.

Another variable used when analyzing power is the
pattern of accommodation in the relationship. Roxanne
Salyer Lulofs (1994) encourages exploration of who is
the most accommodating in the relationship and what
the possibilities are for change, noting particularly
which person labels the conflict. Lulofs (1994)
suggests,

> Generally, people with less power accom-
> modate more and are asked to change more
> radically than those with more power.

> Powerful people accommodate less, have the
> opportunity to label the conflict or define its
> parameters, and have the least interest in
> ensuring that the resolution of the conflict
> meets the needs of all the parties involved
> (p. 158).

As mediators treat each of the parties with dignity and respect, an example is set for how parties can listen to and treat each other—in other words, a model for interaction is established. If one party seems to be accommodating or "caving in," a mediator can gently probe the consequences and implications of the "submission," making sure the decision is a responsible and realistic one.

Conflict is inevitable in our lives. The perspective each person holds concerning conflict often dictates the outcome of disagreements. Ineffective, frustrating, and unproductive outcomes often occur when people see conflict as a contest, with a powerful winner and a not-so-powerful loser. Thomas Crum (1987) uses the metaphor of a "big scoreboard in the heavens" to describe the contest in our lives. People work very hard to be right, to win, or to be the most powerful so they can be ahead in the contest. Thomas Crum (1987) expands on this view of conflict in his book, *The Magic of Conflict.*

> Conflict is not a Contest.
> Winning and losing are goals for games, not
> for conflicts.
> Learning, growing, and cooperating are
> goals for resolving conflicts.
> Conflict can be seen as a gift of energy, in
> which neither side loses and a new dance is
> created.

Resolving conflict is rarely about who is right. It *is* about acknowledgement and appreciation of differences. (p. 49)

In mediation, the two parties are not in a contest. The goal is not to find out who is right, who is to blame, or to whom to give credit. The goal is to find the appropriate resolution to the conflict, one that satisfies both parties. If the participants feel they can safely "let go" of the need to be right or to "win" or to be ahead on the scoreboard, they can move more easily toward exploring options toward agreement in the problem area.

Journal Entry

There's so little that I've been good at in life, that when I found out I was good at fighting, I pursued it with a vengeance. Mediation has given me an opportunity to see how others try to win in a healthy way. It's given me a chance to teach people a way of resolving things without beating the hell out of each other.

Most people feel the need to have at least moderate control of their lives. Gershen Kaufman and Lev Raphael (1983) see this type of power as offering choices for life's decisions. Having choices means the ability to control or to influence conflict situations. Kaufman and Raphael state,

A sense of inner control is the felt experience of power, and having choice over matters which affect us is its wellspring. We must feel able to affect our environment, to feel consulted, to feel we have an impact, to feel heard by those with whom we are in a relationship. To experience choice is to know power. (p. ix)

The mediation process empowers individuals by giving them choices. Many mediation programs require voluntary entry. This entry signals the first choice—to participate or not. Many other choices occur in mediation, including which options to explore, which emotions to show, and the choice to agree on a solution.

The following chapters propose an exploration of mediation as a dispute resolution option that allows conflict to be an opportunity for individuals. Special emphasis is given to the use, misuse, importance of, and place for power considerations within the process. Besides the advantages of this process—the savings of time, energy, and money when resolving disputes—there exists a larger view of mediation. The mediation process is a new language, a way of approaching life, which can help us discover answers to our individual and societal problems. Moving from competitive to cooperative problem solving is a shift of great magnitude, producing opportunities for significant growth and change in today's world.

Chapter 1

Conflict Management

Journal Entry

The most significant conflicts in my life have always occurred in the same context: interpersonal relationships. Learning to identify that all conflicts have basically the same components helps give me the confidence that I have the ability to deal with all of them.

Understanding Conflict

How do you view conflict? When you see or hear the word, are your first responses "pain," "trouble," "fighting," or "misery"? If so, you are not alone. The connotation most people have of conflict is a negative one. Studying mediation provides a larger, less polarized perspective, one which contains opportunities for constructive problem solving and a positive connotation to conflict.

Many conflicts remain negative because individuals do not have the tools to channel differences into a positive or constructive direction. The mediation process offers a channel for learning and implementing the communication skills necessary for this movement to occur. In their book, *Managing Inter-*

7

personal Conflict, William A. Donohue and Robert Kolt (1992) explore the potential for constructive conflict. They use the Chinese symbol for "crisis" on the cover of the book. This symbol has two components, one representing "danger" and one representing "opportunity." Conflict can be dangerous when our needs are threatened and our desires aren't realized—yet an opportunity exists to clarify issues and feelings while taking a step to prevent future conflicts. This chapter explores the dangers and opportunities in conflict and introduces the conflict management strategies commonly used, concluding with a brief explanation of options available for disputes.

EXERCISE
"Conflict Connotations"

In a large group or in small groups, list the **first** words that come to mind when you hear the word "conflict." Circle the words that have a positive connotation with one color marker and the words with a negative connotation with another color marker.
- Are there more words of one connotation than another?
- Continue the discussion by brainstorming for words that lessen the disparity.

Defining Conflict

Although there are numerous definitions of conflict (which is understandable, since disputes exist in a continuum) ranging from interpersonal situations to international crises, many of the components of the definition remain constant. Joyce Hocker and William Wilmot (1991) see conflict as:

> an expressed struggle between at least two interdependent parties who perceive incompatible goals, scarce resources, and interference from the other party in achieving their goals. (p. 12)

Consider the following situation in light of the above definition. Roommates Sue and Jane want to keep the kitchen clean, yet Jane wants to do the dishes weekly while Sue wants them done daily. By using the definition above to explore Sue and Jane's conflict, we see opportunities and dangers.

Expressed struggle: Both parties must realize there is a disagreement for there to be a conflict. If Sue had the desire for daily dishwashing but had never made her desire known, Jane would not be aware of the conflict.

Interdependence: Whether we are dealing with countries, companies, families, or friends in a conflict situation, the parties are usually dependent on each other. Their relationship necessitates communication, and their differences produce conflict. If Jane and Sue were not roommates sharing one kitchen, dishwashing duties would not be an issue for them.

Perceived incompatible goals: In a conflict situation, it usually seems that there will be a winner and a loser. Sue and Jane perceive that they cannot each get what they want. Jane sees her plan as incompatible with Sue's and vice versa.

Perceived scarce rewards: Individuals often see their time, energy, money and other resources as being in limited supply. When there isn't enough of these to go around, conflict can occur. Jane sees no block of time where she could manage daily dishwashing duties, whereas Sue does not want the daily discomfort of seeing a sink full of dirty dishes.

Interference: Sue sees Jane as interfering with her goal of a clean kitchen; Jane sees Sue as interfering with how she spends her time.

Donohue and Kolt (1992) add that conflicts can be manifest or latent. Manifest conflict is out in the open and clearly seen or heard. If Sue leaves Jane a note saying "This kitchen is a mess," and later that day Jane tells Sue "Who has time to do dishes?" manifest conflict exists. Latent conflict exists when people avoid the issue and do not make their discomfort or displeasure apparent. These latent conflicts are often more intrapersonal (within oneself) as the individual struggles with a situation while avoiding bringing it into the open. The expression of this conflict may be internal and may have external manifestations. For example, a man distressed over a workplace relationship may not share it with anyone yet may begin doing sloppy work with a careless attitude.

With a clearer definition of conflict situations, individuals can begin to take steps to promote constructive conflict management. This knowledge can empower individuals when they realize they are taking action to alleviate problems rather than simply hoping a disturbing situation "goes away" or feeling buffeted by events beyond their control.

Words of the Wise

You would think that understanding and handling conflict would be a major priority in our lives. Yet we rarely attempt to understand it. We try to avoid it or resist it. But it always comes back to haunt us. Have you ever avoided keeping adequate financial records only to find yourself paying for it in time and money at tax time? Or have you ever resisted a healthy exercise or nutrition program only to regret it each time you glance in the mirror? How many times have you avoided telling an uncomfortable truth only to find the problem magnified with time, making the eventual telling much more difficult?

Thomas E. Crum (p. 30)

EXERCISE
"Conflict Journal"

Keep a log of the various conflict situations in which you find yourself or you read about or observe. Write about these situations using a two-column format:

- Column 1—Describe the event or situation, being as objective as possible. Pretend you are a disinterested third party observing the conflict. What happened or is happening?
- Column 2—Record your feelings, thoughts, and ideas concerning the conflict. This includes your own subjective evaluations and judgements concerning the situation. Is this situation fair, just, disconcerting, joyous, curious?

These journal entries will give you experience separating the objective from the subjective, a useful skill for mediators.

Managing Conflict

If we are aware that conflict can be constructive or destructive depending on how we handle it or how we use communication tools, it is possible to see a variety of choices in how to manage conflict. Tools we use to encourage effective communication, to be explored throughout this book, include: active listening (listening that displays an intent to understand the intended message), reflecting (acknowledging the emotion in a statement or situation), reframing (reconceptualizing a situation to gain shared understanding), attentive nonverbal behavior, and perception checking (whether we see this situation with the same understanding as others). Five strategies—avoidance, accommodation, competition, compromise, and collaboration—are common choices in dealing with conflict situations in daily life. Each strategy will be defined, possible advantages and disadvantages examined, and an example given for illustration.

Avoidance

Individuals in conflict often decide to avoid the problem area altogether. They are unwilling or unable to face the situation and they "vacate" themselves physically, verbally, or nonverbally. This approach can be useful if the conflict is short-lived (someone's sprinkler splashes water on you while jogging by) or minor (waitress refilled your water glass when you said you'd had enough water). For other situations, the drawbacks to avoiding conflict are many: the conflict can escalate, the relationship most likely will not improve, there will still be an issue "stewing" inside the person, and that person passed up a chance to experience a learning opportunity which could be useful for future conflict. An example of avoidance occurs when a part-time employee avoids speaking up about an unhealthy working environment. He or she could avoid physically (quit the job without telling his or her boss why), verbally (continue answering queries about the working conditions by saying "everything is just fine"), or nonverbally (not say a word and continue to work). The most frequent outcome of avoidance is a perception of a winner and a loser—and a large power imbalance.

Journal Entry

I was incredibly offended and mad. The remarks were bad enough, but speaking to me like I should understand and agree complicated my feelings and made it personal. I very nearly unleashed a torrent of verbal abuse of my own. Instead, I stayed silent. I didn't know what to do. I felt like I was avoiding in a big way, but I didn't think creating a "scene" with someone I work with in the middle of a busy shift was the thing to do. I have done nothing so far but it still disturbs me.

Accommodation

A person who puts the other person's needs or desires ahead of his or her own is accommodating that person. Individuals who fail to assert themselves by always giving in seem to be saying that the other's desires are more important than their own. Sometimes it is just too risky to speak up, as in a case where the consequences may be detrimental. Also, as in avoidance, if the situation just isn't that important, it may be easier for all involved to put one party's desires first. If a father is interested in watching a news program and a son wants some help on an important project for school the next day, the dad can accommodate by helping with the son's project, knowing he can watch the news later.

Accommodation can be detrimental if one person doesn't value the worth or importance of his/her own needs. If a husband always refuses invitations to attend hockey games despite being an avid fan because he thinks his wife will resent being home alone, he is being too accommodating. He is also reacting to a *perceived* conflict. If he doesn't discuss the issue, he may have attributed feelings to his wife that do not exist; that is, he may have misread the situation. Accommodating in this situation and many others may result in a win/lose situation. When an individual accommodates out of low self-confidence or lack of communication skills, that person is doing a disservice to him- or herself.

Competition

Competitive approaches to conflict often involve highly assertive and even aggressive individuals who see conflict as a win/lose situation. One person, usually the more powerful, wins at the other's expense. Competition is a strategy which has its place in clearly defined situations. For example, in a negotiation over the sale of a used car, one party may be bargaining competitively and expects the other party to do the same or risk being perceived as weak or unskilled.

Unless both parties freely define a situation as requiring healthy competition, competitive approaches to conflict can provoke defensiveness in the other party. One person may feel that his or her needs are threatened and will shift the focus of the conflict away from the original issue to combat perceived threats, attacks, and comparisons. Defending oneself becomes the issue, and there is little chance of resolving the first disagreement. The power struggle that occurs in this situation can change a simple conflict into a multi-issue crisis. Two workers who began discussing the issue of "who gets to use the fax machine first" can find themselves in a battle over "who gets a better salary" and "who treats the customers better."

Words of the Wise

Ultimately, however, conflict lies not in objective reality, but in people's heads. Truth is simply one more argument—perhaps a good one, perhaps not—for dealing with the difference. The difference itself exists because it exists in their thinking. Fears, even if ill-founded, are real fears and need to be dealt with.

Hopes, even if unrealistic, may cause a war. Facts,
even if established, may do nothing to solve the
problem.
                            Roger Fisher & William Ury (p. 23)

Compromise

When two parties meet halfway in negotiation, both
give up something they want or need and meet
somewhere in the middle. Because individuals give up
a part of their wants or needs, compromise is
sometimes seen as a lose/lose situation. Compromise
can be effective in a situation where you have a multifaceted issue and time is short. If two countries are
negotiating about a cease-fire and they need an
immediate decision, they may each strike three of their
requests and agree on one. This approach can also be
useful if both parties have tried collaborating (see next
section) and the negotiation has fallen apart. When
these two countries have worked together for two
months with no clear results, they may decide to
compromise for the time being until a more appropriate negotiation situation can be arranged.

The disadvantage of this strategy is that both parties
often leave the negotiation dissatisfied. It may have
been mutually acceptable to end the negotiation this
way, but it may not have been mutually acceptable to
settle on the compromised terms.

Collaboration

The goal of a collaborative style of conflict management is to produce a win/win situation. Both parties
are attempting to satisfy the needs and/or desires of
each side. Collaboration requires a commitment from

each side, a desire to work together and to produce a solution that is mutually acceptable. The first hurdle is to reach a mutually agreeable assessment of the issue to be confronted.

Collaboration is most advantageous to people who want to preserve an ongoing relationship—whether spouses, employee-employer, neighbors, or office mates. Collaboration allows parties to experience creative and constructive problem solving, which can be an opportunity to prevent the next conflict. Consider the situation where a landlord wants to raise the rent to pay for building upkeep and the tenant is unable to pay more. A collaborative negotiation could result in the landlord deciding not to raise the rent as the tenant (a carpenter) agrees to help paint and repair.

Use of collaboration may be risky in some cases, as in the case of the negotiator who initiates with collaboration and then switches to competition. Occasionally, a party may seem to be "working with" the other party on a complicated issue. In the end, it is evident that the first party was merely using collaboration to gather information to gain power to "go for the big win."

Collaborative approaches to conflict management are often win/win situations. Parties work to explore options to resolution that can satisfy both of them. A mutually acceptable, collaborative resolution is usually not a spectacular one for either party, but is reasonable, workable, and satisfying.

EXERCISE
"Rock, Paper, Scissors"

Remember the game with this name? Each party mentally chooses rock, paper, or scissors and then when the choice is discovered, there are winners and losers. This exercise is similar in that participants choose **avoidance, accommodation, compromise, competition, or collaboration** (mentally) and then participate in a role play using that conflict management style. This works the best in dyads. The following role plays can be used:

1. Two employees, a smoker and a nonsmoker, discuss creation of a new policy regarding smoking at the workplace.
2. A teacher discusses a failing grade with a protesting student.
3. Two parents try to decide on discipline decisions for a son who has been staying out very late at night.
4. Two neighboring countries discuss border control. Discussion can revolve around issues like:
   - How did your style feel to you?
   - How did the other person's style affect you?
   - Which style was most comfortable/uncomfortable for you?
   - Were you ever tempted to switch styles in the midst of a role play? Why?
   - How did these styles affect the **power** of the participants?

Conflict management implies an ongoing concern, both for the individual conflict situation and the larger situation in which it occurs. Managing this situation supposes that we are not just resolving problems to make room for new problems, but at the same time creating an environment that may effectively diagnose, work through, and perhaps prevent future conflicts.

Seeing an option in conflict management not just to solve problems but also to transform people and situations is the foundation of the book *The Promise of Mediation: Responding to Conflict Through Empowerment and Recognition*, by Robert Baruch Bush and Joseph Folger (1994). These authors contend that as people change during the conflict management process, they develop positive capabilities to deal with differences and challenges. Bush and Folger see mediation and other conflict management processes in our society today as moving toward a more "problem solving" approach—finding solutions and creating specific settlements. The "transformative" approach suggests that if we empower parties to define issues and settlement terms for themselves, parties can better understand each other's perspectives and can create more genuine solutions to their problems.

The mediation model presented later in this text follows a more transformative approach to conflict management. The goal of the process is not only to have a resolution (in which case the term "conflict resolution" would be more appropriate), but the goal is to transform the parties during a mediation process that uses this definition of empowerment, recognition and success:

Empowerment: strengthened self-awareness
Recognition: expanded willingness to acknowledge and be responsive to other
parties' situations and human qualities
Success:
(1) if the parties have been made aware of the
opportunities presented during the mediation
for both empowerment and recognition;
(2) if the parties have been helped to clarify
goals, options, and resources, and then to
make informed, deliberate and free choices
regarding how to proceed at every decision
point; and
(3) if the parties have been helped to give
recognition wherever it was their decision to
do so. (Bush & Folger, 1994, pp. 84–85)

Resolving Disputes

A term that is often used in the discussion of
conflict is "dispute." When parties have identified the
underlying issues or the unique component of the
conflict they wish to resolve, they have identified the
dispute. Donohue and Kolt (1992) see a dispute as
more than a problem to solve; it is a needs-centered
conflict—who needs what and at what cost to whom?
While the conflict for Sue and Jane concerns a "clean
kitchen," the dispute is about who will do the dishes
and when.

The first decision that needs to be made when
facing a dispute is whether the two parties can *negotiate* a resolution to their dispute or if they need the
assistance of a third party. The remaining section of
this chapter concerns five different strategies for
dispute resolution: negotiation, conciliation, mediation,

arbitration, and adjudication. All but the negotiation process require the help of a third party.

Negotiation

When two parties engage in discussion attempting to reach an agreement, they are using the process of negotiation. This process allows maximum empowerment of the disputing parties, as they have complete control of the situation. A challenge to this process arises when the parties are not using the same conflict management strategy. It is important to identify which strategy each party is using and whether they share the same goal concerning resolution of the issues.

Gerald Williams (1983) sees negotiators as being either aggressive or cooperative. The aggressive negotiators use "value-claiming" tactics—the more competitive or win/lose strategies. Aggressive negotiators claim their side has more worth. The cooperative negotiators use "value-creating" tactics. These negotiators seek a common ground and a fair solution, creating a valuable solution together. Whether the parties choose one of the strategies mentioned earlier, or whether they create a new process, a successful negotiation involves a show of good faith on both sides. When parties negotiate in good faith, they both exhibit the desire to work through their differences and to make an agreement on a specific issue. Getting to "good faith" negotiation is sometimes difficult, and the negotiators may need to request the assistance of a third party.

Conciliation

When a neutral third party helps disputing parties with relational issues, an informal and highly flexible process occurs. The disputants still maintain a high degree of control over the process. The conciliator helps to lower tensions, improve communication, and explore possible solutions. Individuals involved in divorce often use conciliation to help them get to a manageable place in their relationship so they can proceed with content issues.

Conciliation can bring parties to the point where they agree to mediate, negotiate, or arbitrate. Specific programs, usually religious or counseling, often offer a conciliation step. This is often mistakenly referred to as mediation. Conciliation stops short of mediation but may set the scene for mediation. By attempting to clarify misconceptions and reduce unreasonable fears, conciliators encourage parties to go on to a face-to-face discussion, either with a third party or as a negotiation.

Mediation

When a neutral third party facilitates a negotiation where disputants discuss their differences, identify areas of agreement, and test options with a possible outcome being mutually acceptable resolution, mediation occurs. Mediators focus on more than relational problems. They look at specific content issues and encourage the parties to create their own solutions to the problem areas. Often two mediators work as a team to comprise the "neutral third party."

The parties in this process are in control of the information and issues discussed while the mediator keeps control of the process. Mediators are often called "process facilitators" or "process managers" because they impose flexible rules on the process that make it more formal than conciliation. In a divorce mediation, the parties may deal with division of property and custody settlement (content), as well as relationship problems that need to be resolved (relational). In a workplace situation, two employees may mediate concerning long-distance telephone calls (content) and communication styles when discussing workplace issues (relational).

The qualifications for becoming a mediator vary from state to state, with the basic requirement usually being completion of the nationally recognized forty-hour Basic Training program which deals with the topics presented in this text. Mediation programs with specific focuses may encourage the mediator to have specialized specific training or to possess expertise in a particular area. For example, a family mediation program may want mediators to have a psychology or counseling degree in addition to the forty-hour training. A divorce mediation office often uses a lawyer/psychologist combination for the unique issues that may arise. A university mediation program for student issues may want mediators to have a broad knowledge of communication effectiveness, in order to model skills for the students to use in their own conflict management. A mediation program dealing with land-use disputes may want a mediator who is an expert in community and regional planning. Finally, many mediation programs want mediators skilled in the mediation process without requiring specific, substantive knowledge about the issue, allowing for the neutral third party to facilitate without biases that may interfere with the process.

Journal Entry

We need to get the message out to the public about what mediation is, as opposed to other dispute resolution processes. I have seen articles in the paper and heard references in other places to mediations "won or lost." This public perception should be considered. Without distinguishing mediation from these kinds of win/lose concepts, where will mediation end up? Could mediation become another legalistic, court-related process?

Arbitration

Arbitration is a form of private judging where two parties grant a third party control over the outcome in a dispute. The arbitrator hears all sides of the dispute, reviews the evidence, and issues a decision, which may or may not be legally binding. This is usually a more rigid structure with more formal rules. Arbitration often ignores relational problems and underlying issues. The parties do not decide the outcome; they have much less power in this process. If a divorce case were heard in arbitration, the arbitrator might tell the parties how much property each gets and who gets custody of the children, etc. The section below implies that arbitration is *not* legally binding—in some cases it *is* (baseball salaries, for example).

Adjudication

Adjudication, or "going to court," can be an effective last-resort option when trying to find a final solution to a problem. It is similar to arbitration with the exception of the outcome—a final, legally binding solution decided by an adjudicator (judge or jury). This process is the most formal of the third-party intervention choices and contains specific rules and procedures. Since adjudication is an adversarial process, attorneys often represent the disputing parties.

Choosing a Dispute Resolution Strategy

Disputing parties who are interested in selecting a third-party intervention must consider all available options. The following questions can help deal with that choice:

- What goals do we have? (Typical goals may be: (1) a quick, easy resolution of the problem, (2) preserving a relationship, (3) preventing problems from escalating).
- What issues do we want to deal with? Content? Relationship? Both?
- How formal of a process do we want to work with? (Do we want to sit comfortably on a sofa with a cup of tea or do we want to be afforded the formality of a courtroom or conference room?)
- How much power or control do we want over the process or the outcome? (Do we want to speak for ourselves or have someone speak for us?)

- What are the time, energy, and financial considerations?

When parties adhere to the view that conflict is negative, they rush into methods of resolution that enable them to "make it go away" or to "get it over quickly." With a positive view of conflict, one which envisions constructive results, individuals can carefully choose a dispute resolution method that suits them and the conflict.

Words of the Wise

Well-planned confrontations work out much better than unplanned ones. How much time should you spend planning? Consider the slogan, "There never seems to be enough time to do the job right but always time to do it over." Planning asks that you invest your time on the front end of the problem as opposed to the back end. Waiting until the problem grows large requires significantly more repair work than a little routine maintenance up front.

W. A. Donohue with R. Kolt (p. 47)

Chapter 2

Mediation: An Overview

Mediation is emerging as a preferable means to manage differences in our relationships, families, workplaces, schools, communities and institutions. Within Alternative Dispute Resolution (a movement designed to create alternatives to litigation), mediation seems to have "come of age" (Pearce & Littlejohn, in press). As a method for bringing interested parties together to work out their differences, mediation provides opportunities for people to find workable solutions that satisfy the interests of all parties. Agreements can be reached sooner and through a less costly process than most other alternatives. Agreements are often more easily implemented in comparison to verdicts and third-party directed decisions.

Although mediation has long been used in labor disputes, Bush and Folger (1994) point out that the last twenty-five years have seen a remarkable growth and development in the field of mediation. It is important to view mediation in comparison to the other dispute resolution processes (negotiation, conciliation, arbitration, and adjudication). As a process that affords the disputing individuals a greater amount of power, mediation is seen as especially desirable to underrepresented or low-power parties. Further, individuals who are interested in having control of the outcome in a dispute usually prefer this process.

In a broad sense, mediation encompasses a form of communication where barriers are broken down and bridges are built. The mediator, as a neutral third party, focuses discussions and helps shape the language used, with a goal of coming up with a mutually acceptable solution. This process opens communication channels and creates an atmosphere for problem solving. More specifically, *mediation is a process where parties are encouraged to see and make clear, deliberate choices, while acknowledging the perspective of the other. In this process, mutually acceptable agreement is one possible outcome.* This text presents the stages of the process from the introduction to story telling, then problem solving, and finally the resolution stage. Mediation extends the negotiation process by asking a third party to monitor the process while allowing the principals responsibility for their own resolution to the conflict.

Words of the Wise

We have come to believe that mediation's greatest value lies in its potential not only to find solutions to people's problems but to change people themselves for the better, in the very midst of conflict. Time and again, we have seen people change in small but significant ways through their participation in this process. These changes occur because, through mediation, people find ways to avoid succumbing to conflict's most destructive pressures: to act from weakness rather than

strength and to de-humanize rather than acknowledge each other.
                    R. A. Baruch Bush & J. P. Folger (p. xv)

Role of the Mediator

The mediator is a facilitator who manages the dispute resolution process. Unlike a judge or an arbitrator who makes decisions for the party, the mediator remains impartial and neutral. Being impartial does not mean a mediator is without opinions or perceptions. Rather, he or she is alert to biases and prejudices, while having the ability to put them aside so they do not affect or alter the process or the outcome.

It is helpful to use the metaphor of a tape recorder when conceptualizing neutrality in mediation. If we think of ourselves as having running tape recorders throughout our lives, we can imagine the vast amounts of information we have stored. Our experiences, teachings, travels, observations, readings, and thoughts are all stored and recalled in certain situations. Think of *all* of the parties in a mediation with their own tape recording of experiences, perceptions and biases ready to be used as evidence. A mediator, aware of all this divergent stored information, makes a conscious decision to **turn off the recordings, to the best of his or her abilities,** during the mediation process.

Neutrality is also an attitude and a behavior manifested by the mediator. Most often, the mediator professes no relationship with the parties that could affect the outcome. If there is such a relationship between the mediator and one of the parties, it should not benefit one at the other's expense.

It has often been stated that one of the duties of a mediator is to "balance power" between the parties. A more accurate description is to see the mediator as one who attempts to empower each individual party. "Balancing power" is like comparing mediation to a see-saw. In this view, the mediator acts as the fulcrum, adjusting to balance the weight (power) of two unequally weighted individuals. This metaphor implies a judgement on the part of the media-tor—deciding which party holds more or less power.

A more appropriate metaphor would be to deal with each individual as a mediator would deal with the emperor in the tale *The Emperor's New Clothes*. No one dares tell the emperor that he is naked (using the conflict management strategy of avoidance). While a judge or arbitrator may reach a verdict of "You're naked," the mediator creates a safe environment and, using communication tools, allows the emperor to save face and realize his condition on his own. This empowering step allows the process to keep moving forward without causing the parties to become defensive or embarrassed.

The mediation process and strategies used by mediators address the need for parties to "save face." As discussed in chapter 5, "face" is the image that a person portrays in public and most often used to protect one's greatest vulnerabilities. Mediators can guide parties through a sensitive process with little damage to their image. To do so, mediators must be skilled at identifying possible "minefields" for both parties. By guiding discussions around issues most likely to raise defense mechanisms, the mediator can keep all the available energy focused on the content issue.

It is important to remember that a mediator does not function as a judge, a counselor, an advocate, or a lawyer. Kolb and Associates (1994) warn that mediator "power" can be viewed with distrust and some wariness. They note that "by keeping a low profile and getting the parties to do the lion's share of the work, a mediator avoids the risk of becoming another party with an agenda to pursue" (p. 477). Keeping in mind that the ultimate responsibility for resolution rests on the disputants, mediators can remain clear on their roles.

Benefits

Mediation helps build solutions that are reasonable, efficient, and effective. When resolution options are identified by the parties, the mediator encourages focused scrutiny to make sure the solution is workable and realistic for both parties. Mediators question the options, suggestions, and solutions offered by the disputing parties to anticipate any problems with the suggested direction.

The mediation process saves time, energy, and finances, especially when compared to adjudication. Little or no time is spent in prior investigation or preparation of documents. Compared to court and attorney's fees, mediation is usually quite affordable. Participants in mediation may pay a small filing fee ($5–$25), using a process with volunteer mediators—a common occurrence in small claims court and community mediation. Private mediators charge as much as $200 an hour, depending on experience, expertise, or program considerations.

The effectiveness of mediation can be seen by the often high rate of adherence to the resolution—and by the improved communication between the parties as a result of participating in the process. When both parties agree to a resolution *they* created, they feel ownership of the agreement—resulting in the willingness and desire to implement the resolution. The University of New Mexico Mediation Clinic embraces this concept with their motto, "People support what they create."

Another important aspect of mediation is early intervention in conflict. Attention to issues early in the conflict can de-escalate the problem before it is unmanageable. What may seem like a minor dispute—not worth inputting time and energy into—may actually offer the best opportunity to avoid irreparable schisms. Individual conflict handling styles can be recognized and accommodation for them incorporated into the process before they become so ingrained that no alternatives are possible. Early intervention, when disputes are more likely confined to a single issue, has a better chance of producing the mutually satisfactory, win/win solutions than a full-blown crisis has.

Uses

Mediation techniques can be implemented at many points along the conflict resolution continuum. If its approach to conflict as opportunity for learning, growing, and cooperating is internalized, its principles can be used in intrapersonal communication (talking to yourself), and interpersonal communication (one-on-one communication) with schools, families, companies, governments, cities, and countries. Mediation language will be evident in a multitude of situations where conflict is likely to occur. Whether a student learns mediation skills in a university setting, in a workshop, at a church, in a business, or through participation in a mediation process, these skills are directly transferable to other settings. The following are examples of some uses of mediation seen today:

- court-connected small claims mediation
- victim-offender mediation in the juvenile justice system
- divorce mediation (concerning property, custody, finances, etc.)
- church mediation (healing divisive church conflicts)
- school conflict management (peer mediation)
- employer-employee (work-related disputes)
- attorney as mediator (attempt to settle before court)
- city development (facilitate issues between developer, neighborhood, and city)
- international disputes (boundaries, cease-fires, civil)

When Mediation Is Effective

As you see in the above list, mediation can be considered in situations where there is a relationship involved, particularly one that is long lasting. If parties are to mediate successfully, they need some degree of communication competence. They need minimal communication skills and the ability to follow

some degree of structure, as provided by the mediation process and the resulting agreement. Parties need
to have some desire to work through the problem.
There are some conditions that make settlement in
mediation more easily achievable. Successful mediation can still occur without these conditions, but
cases that include these components will be settled
more frequently (Moore, 1989):

• a previous history of cooperation
• no long history of dispute, distrust, litigation
• a reasonable number of issues in the dispute
• moderate or low hostility towards each other
• external pressure to settle (for example, one
  party faces a time constraint)
• limited psychological attachment toward each
  other
• adequate resources that can be divided

Mediation can also be effective if all of the parties
involved are conscious of the goals. Jeff Grant, a
mediator in New Mexico, believes that most parties
will have a goal of resolution. However, this "resolution" may be very broad. To some, it may mean
simply being heard, to others it may mean job security, while to others it may mean getting a good
night's sleep. The goal of the process is to support the
negotiation between the disputants as they move
toward resolution. The goal of the mediator is to set
guidelines that provide safety and balance for the
parties involved and to assist each party in understanding him- or herself and the other party. According to Grant, the only reason the mediator needs
to know what the dispute is about is to understand
the flow of conversation and to help the parties sort
out their feelings about the issues. One of the most

important jobs of the mediator is to identify the differing goals that must flow together before a solution can be reached.

Remembering that conflict is normal and inevitable, mediators can help individuals work through their disputes while offering behaviors and language to be mirrored and utilized in any relationship. The mediation model can be a powerful tool for healing the anxiety that often accompanies conflict and implementing fair solutions. Success is attained when a mediator uses effective communication techniques to facilitate a process where individuals become more cooperative negotiators.

EXERCISE
"Dismantle the Definition"
(contributed by Jeff Grant)

Using the following definition of mediation, experiment with removing components and note what kind of process results.

Mediation: A confidential, voluntary process where a neutral third party facilitates negotiation between two or more parties with mutually acceptable agreement as one possible outcome.

- Remove one word or phrase from the definition. How does this change the definition?
- Does this change make the process similar to any of the other dispute resolution processes?
- How would this change affect the participants? The mediators? Society?

Chapter 3

Stages of Mediation

Many trainers, writers, and teachers have delineated the stages of a mediation process. Whether consisting of seven steps, five steps, or four steps (as presented here), most agree that the stages of mediation are fluid, flexible, and part of a process. Mediation trainer Cynthia Olson believes that mediators need to be embedded in the process. In fact, she points out that knowledge of the process is more important than substantive knowledge. When speaking of "leaning on the process," mediators are trusting these stages to bring the parties toward resolution. There are times when this process takes ten minutes (as when the parties needed five minutes of venting before they felt free to resolve) or many hours (with complicated, multifaceted issues or strong positional perspectives). Whatever the situation, mediation is most successful when using a process that includes the four components presented by Roger Fisher and William Ury in their book, *Getting To Yes: Negotiating Agreement Without Giving In.*

Fisher and Ury use a strategy developed at Harvard Negotiation Project called "Principled Negotiation," where issues are decided on their merits while looking for mutual gains. The following four principles comprise this method of resolving conflict:

1. **Separate the people from the problem**
   When two parties are very positional (that is, having predetermined a particular stance) in their view of the conflict, the relationship and the content of the conflict often get confused. It is important to separate the people (relationship, personalities) from the problem (facts, content, substance). Deal with the people as human beings and deal with the problem on its merits.

2. **Focus on interests, not positions**
   The interests behind positions are the needs, desires, concerns, and fears that caused the party to adopt that position. Often, behind seemingly incompatible positions one finds shared interests. By reconciling these interests, rather than compromising on positions, a mutually advantageous solution can result.

   The well-used example of an orange illustrates this. Two siblings were fighting over the last orange in the fruit basket. Their mother could have made a quick decision either to split the orange or to give the orange to the child who had the cleanest room or who had been the most respectful that day. If the mother had taken a minute to explore WHY each child wanted the orange, she may have found that they had compatible interests. One child wanted the peel of the orange to feed the hamster, and the other wanted a snack. Compatible interests often lie beneath seemingly incompatible positions.

3. **Invent options for mutual gain**
   When two parties are negotiating, they often have the assumption of a "fixed pie." The perception is that there is only a certain amount of "pie" (time,

finances, assets, resources), and if one wins or gets more, the other loses or gets less. The principle suggested here is to *assume* a larger pie. Negotiators can expand the pie by inventing options *before* dividing it. This creative expansion can produce a much larger range of options with benefits for each side.

4. **Insist on using objective criteria**

   When settling differences in positions and interests, it is often important to look at solutions on the basis of objective criteria, independent of either side. This approach encourages the parties to commit themselves to reaching a solution based on principle, not pressure. By accepting fair standards and methods of testing the reality of options, a fair and acceptable outcome results.

EXERCISE
"Interests Underlying Positions"

Write down five of your most strongly held positions. For each of these positions, list three or four possible interests, principles, and/or values that contributed to forming that position. Note the primary interest that truly motivates you to hold the position. (Be aware that others may attribute your position to other interests.)

Journal Entry

The problem is that both sides are so locked into their positions that it is hard to imagine them committing to any joint problem-solving process. They had

> reached a so-called compromise, but that
> offered only a stopgap, temporary halt to
> the conflict. The compromise did not
> address the needs of either party. No
> one was committed to it, and neither side
> paid any attention to it.

Keeping these four principles in mind, the stages of mediation can be explored: 1) introduction, 2) story-telling stage, 3) problem-solving stage, 4) resolution stage. All the stages can be subdivided into other categories. Indeed, as mentioned earlier, some people see negotiation as a seven-step process. We have chosen to delineate four major steps.

Introduction

The introduction in a mediation session sets the tone for the rest of the process. Do not underestimate the importance of this step or leave it out in an effort to move forward quickly. The introduction has three primary purposes. These purposes provide common ground—a point where the parties can start at the same place, despite their other differences. The introduction 1) introduces the disputants to the mediators and to each other; 2) gives an explanation of the process; and 3) establishes trust.

In most cases, an "agreement to mediate" form has been given to parties (see sample in appendix). The facts on this form can be agreed on and signed by both parties. Usually, a signed form is required before moving forward with the process.

Many mediators either memorize the different parts of the introduction or jot down the points on a

note card to make sure they include everything. The following parts of an introduction are necessary:
1. introduction of mediators and parties
2. words of encouragement
3. explanation of the process
   definition of mediation
   mediator's role
   ground rules
   confidentiality
   caucus (break in the process)
4. ask for questions

A mediator needs to be flexible with these steps, as one of the parties may ask questions or make comments at any time. If the parties relate stories about previous mediations or begin explaining their current situation, the mediators should reassure them that they will have adequate time to explain, in a minute or two, but first they need to hear some necessary information.

This mediation relationship enables the participants to feel comfortable, with the disputants believing that the mediation process can help them. If a trust relationship is created, the disputants can participate openly while seeing the mediator as competent. All components of the introduction work together to set the tone and to establish trust. If a trusting environment is evident from the start, it will facilitate the entire process. People often have misconceptions about mediation, and this is the time to get everyone on the same track. The following steps in the introduction all include trust-building methods.
1. **Introductions**
   When the parties first arrive, it is important to make introductions all around the table. Mediators

usually inquire how the individuals would like to be addressed. Often they respond that it would be OK to use first names. With a large group, it may be helpful to use name-tags or write names on a board or a piece of paper. When mediators introduce themselves, it is helpful to fully describe their position: "I am Maria Lopez, a trained mediator with the Neighborhood Dispute Resolution Center. I am participating here as part of a contract with the Metro Court Mediation Program."

2. **Words of encouragement**
   After everyone has introduced themselves, it is a good opportunity to commend the participants for choosing to use the mediation process. Remind them that it is a valuable dispute-resolution step when people have a hand in resolving their own problems. A mediator can compliment the parties on being willing to meet together and use the mediation process. Just the fact that the parties are in attendance is positive movement toward resolution. These "complimentary" words can also be repeated throughout the process, whenever positive progress is noted.

3. **Explain the process**
   After the appropriate greetings and introductions take place, mediators need to explain the process of mediation as it will be used that day. This definition may include one of the following definitions or it may be a combination of several, as appropriate:
   • a collaborative process that focuses on individual interests and concerns, identifying options, testing expected consequences of

those options, and allowing parties to see the perspective of the other.

- a process where a neutral third party facilitates communication so two parties have the opportunity to come up with a resolution that is mutually satisfactory
- a voluntary process where a mutually acceptable agreement is sought through the guidance of an impartial mediator team
- an interest-based process where a neutral third party facilitates negotiation.
- a facilitated discussion of differences

After defining the mediation process, it is important to explain the role the mediator plays. Often this is done by explaining what a mediator does *not* do: "We are not judges, nor arbiters. We will make no decisions for you or give you advice toward resolving your problem. We will not take sides or advocate either side or position."

It is also helpful to explain what the mediator *does* do: "As neutral third parties, we will facilitate your communication and be in charge only of the process. We will help you discuss your problem with each other and guide you toward managing the problem." Trust can be built as mediators explain their role. The participants can get their first glimpse of the impartiality of the mediators and trust that their interests are important.

After defining mediation and the role of the mediator, another common ground is established by offering *ground rules*. These rules revolve around the theme of "common courtesy." When mentioning courtesy in the process, a mediator is establishing a respectful atmosphere. Only one

person needs to speak at a time, with no interruptions. Name-calling or violent interjections and
disturbances are not welcome in this process and
may precipitate a break, a caucus (see discussion
below), or an end to the session. To avoid
interruptions, participants and mediators can take
notes to remind themselves of a point they want to
bring up later. Mediators can provide pencils and
paper for this purpose.

All participants need to be aware of time
considerations. Someone may need to get back to
work, catch a ride, or get to a child care agency. In
these cases, a mediator needs to make the parties
aware of the options if a mediation is cut short.
Rescheduling should be an acceptable option. If
that is not possible, participants can brainstorm
about what they want to do if time runs out and
the process is not finished.

Explain to the participants that strict
confidentiality will be observed. They need to
know that they are free to air their concerns
without worrying about what an outsider might
think if the particulars of the session were
revealed. For example, participants might hesitate
to criticize the work environment if they fear their
statements will be repeated to managers of the
company. Trust sets the stage for an environment
conducive to creating an agreement that the parties
are comfortable with and are willing to support.
By keeping information from the mediation
confidential, this safe atmosphere can be created.
(See sample confidentiality form in appendix.)

A final point to be explained in the introduction
to the process is the possibility of calling a

"caucus." These separate meetings are not always needed, but occasionally the parties reach an impasse, and the mediators decide to speak to each party individually. The Appendix contains a sample of how all these elements can be presented in the introduction.

4. **Ask for questions**
   Before moving to the story-telling stage, it is important to check if anyone has any questions or concerns. With a final smile of encouragement and acknowledgement that everyone is ready to begin, the mediators start the next stage.

EXERCISE
"Introduction Practice"

In groups of two, take turns practicing a mediation introduction. Use notes to remind yourself about all the components to be discussed.

Story-Telling Stage

This phase of the mediation process is sometimes seen as similar to a litigation session. Each party is invited to give an "opening statement," the first step in identifying the problem. Usually, the mediators ask the person who brought the case to mediation to speak first. Other times the mediators will arbitrarily choose someone to go first. Statements or questions such as, "Let's begin by having each of you describe what you feel is the crux of the problem. Both of you will have the same opportunity, so please don't interrupt to state your position." "Tell us what brought you to mediation," "What is the problem you are confronting?" or "What is happening?" can get the process moving. The participants can be reminded that it would be helpful simply to describe or explain the situation—not to accuse or confront. If the parties interrupt or break the ground rules, the mediators can remind them to take notes concerning what they want to say and to reassure the parties that they will have their time to speak. Sometimes it is useful to encourage the parties to speak to the mediators, rather than to each other, helping reduce anger or tension.

While the parties are explaining their stories, the mediators need to watch and listen carefully. This is the time to begin noting positions and interests. Verbal **and** nonverbal behavior can give lots of information to aid the process. For example, the mediator can listen to how a participant characterizes the problem. Is he or she dividing the issue into an "us" versus "them" conflict? Does the vocabulary indicate a lack of emotional control? Does the participant portray himself or herself as a victim? How much eye contact is there between the two parties or with the mediator? What does the body posture indicate? Submission? Defiance? Does each party listen to the other, or does one or both scribble notes furiously at the first statement made? What word(s) triggered the response?

Ideally, the length of speaking time should be balanced for each party's opening statement. Five to ten minutes each can give parties enough time to present a picture of the problem. If one party seems to be taking too long, the mediators can courteously ask him or her to summarize. If one party does not say much, the mediator can encourage the person to tell more of the story by asking, "What happened next?"

"How did that make you feel?" "Tell me more about . . . (specific incident)."

It is essential for the mediator to remember how important these opening statements are. Often it is only after being given the opportunity to share their **whole** story that parties feel comfortable enough to continue the process. The following listening techniques let the parties know that their stories **are** important.

Listening Techniques

The listening techniques used in the story-telling stage also should be used throughout the rest of the process. The purpose of these techniques in this stage is to let the participants know that both their feelings and the substance of the issue are valid entities to be considered. The mediators are showing respect for the parties, which in turn builds trust in the mediators and in the process.

Listening is an *active* (rather than passive) process, and mediators should attempt to understand the emotions expressed, the substance (facts) of the problem, and what the positions and interests are. Mediators do this by being active participant observers. Attentive posture and respectful eye communication are important indicators of involvement. Mediators can nod their heads, say "uh-huh," and use facial expressions that show an attitude of caring and concern.

While inaccurate perceptions, faulty assumptions, and distractions affect how well we receive incoming messages, there can also be a physical reason for difficulty in listening. Wolvin and Coakley (1992,

p. 243) found that people have spare time to use when they are listening. The average person speaks between 125 and 150 words per minute, while most humans are capable of understanding speech at rates of as many as 500 words per minute. While it is easy to lose concentration during this extra time, mediators can use it to understand the speaker's ideas and to read the nonverbal signals. Without effective listening, the mediator will be unable to summarize, clarify, reframe, and acknowledge elements learned in the introduction and story-telling stages of the mediation process.

EXERCISE
"Active Listening"

In a group setting, brainstorm topics of discussion to find one that would ensure a lively discussion. When the group has chosen a topic that everyone knows something about, begin with a statement of that issue. Group participants cannot give their opinion until they have accurately summarized the previous person's message. Take care to reflect the emotions and feelings as well as reframing the substance or facts of the message. When summarizing a message, it is important to check with the first speaker to determine if the summary was accurate. If not, some clarification may be needed. Continue this discussion until each participant has had a chance to speak and summarize.

The following verbal techniques can assist a mediator when exploring statements in a mediation session.

Summarizing

After each opening statement, it is helpful for mediators to summarize what they have heard. The important issues and facts can be pulled together at this point, establishing a common ground before further discussion ensues. A mediator can begin summarizing statements this way:

- "It sounds like the three main issues you are concerned with are . . ."
- "Let's see if I have this straight; you experienced _____ and feel _____."
- "Let me summarize what I've heard so far."

These statements can produce a basis for further discussion, especially when the participants correct the mediator's assumptions. If a participant does not agree with the summarization, further story telling may be needed.

Summarizing is also a useful tool to review progress in the session. Participants usually like to feel that they are getting somewhere and that this problem-statement period is leading somewhere. Mediators can review progress with statements such as:

- "You've decided that ____ and ____ are not huge problem areas to be dealt with, so let us move on to . . ."
- "It looks like each of you has gotten a lot of new information on this issue. You've gotten a lot clearer picture of the choices before you."

Summarizing is a way to keep a clearer picture available for the participants and the mediators. Some mediators use this technique periodically throughout the whole session to tie together the main points of the story that have surfaced. Even when nearing resolution, it is helpful to summarize the progression thus far in identifying the facts. Participants see this as another respectful measure of assurance that the mediators are concerned with the whole story.

Clarifying

After the opening statements, which are mostly monologues, the process becomes more of an exchange between the participants and the mediators. At this stage, the mediators have heard about the events that precipitated the dispute, and the participants are responding to issues brought up in the opening statements.

The mediators may still need to get more information on specific issues and can often use clarifying statements and questions such as:

- "I'd like some more information about what happened after the incident. Could you share more?"
- "John, how do you respond to Jane's statement that you . . . ?"
- "Pete, can you tell me more about . . . ?"

Mediators must be careful not to appear to be judging the participants or the events. The mediator's questions need to be specific and to the point, keeping the discussion to the issues in question. Obviously, questions like, "How can you have hurt your husband like that?" or "That certainly is not a fair business deal" can provoke defensiveness in the participants.

When clarifying, the type of question used influences the process in different ways. **Closed questions** are those that elicit a "yes," "no," or one-word answer. These questions are useful for confirming a mediator's summarization or establishing a specific point of fact for both parties to acknowledge. These questions are not preferred when exploring an issue for more information. Instead, **open questions** seek more information and invite longer answers. Beginning a question with words like "how" or "what" or "why" (exercising caution so that these statements don't sound accusatory) will encourage more details and more precise identification of the problem. There is sometimes a need to be careful of "why" questions, as they may evoke defensiveness in the participants, thinking that the mediator is asking for justification of actions. The "why" of a question could be inserted further into the statement, such as, "I'd like some more information as to why you are feeling that way." When mediators use clarifying tools, they are implying that what has been said has value. Besides stating to participants that they are concerned with the whole story, mediators model a quest for clear information about both facts and feelings.

Reframing

A mediator reframes a situation or a statement by redefining or reconceptualizing it verbally. Reframing improves communication between the parties and helps the mediators check on the actual intended message. Reframing also puts the message into language that may be easier for the other party and mediators to understand. When mediators reframe, they let the speaker know that they grasp the facts. By restating the basic ideas, mediators put the message into easy-to-understand language, such as, "In other words, what happened is . . ." or "So, your idea is to . . ."

Some more specific ways that mediators use reframing are to:

- **identify commonalities**—"I see you are both interested in security";
- **increase or decrease the level of emotion**—"It looks like you have some extremely strong feelings about dishonesty";
- **bring out the interests beneath the positions**—"I recognize that you want to make money and secure your reputation."

Using a technique that redefines an issue, mediators can help the process move toward resolution. As parties see the issues more clearly and begin to note commonalities, they are inclined to have confidence in and to continue the process.

Reflecting

A strength of the mediation process is attention to the emotional or feeling component to a dispute or conflict. Many models of conflict resolution put effort only into dealing with the content (facts, evidence). Mediation encourages exploration of the feelings associated with the conflict.

A tool that mediators use to convey the message that emotions are an important part of the process is

reflection of feelings. By listening to the feelings (stated or implied) underlying the content, mediators can echo the emotions and check to see if their impressions are accurate. Reflection of feelings can occur at any stage in the process. One disputant tells the following story:

> My daughter continually shuts me out of her life. Every time I try to talk to her, she either walks away or gives me a dirty look. I have begged her to talk to me, bribed her with new clothes, and ordered her to be more respectful. She just hates me!

Mediators can respond to just the feelings, giving a reflection: "It sounds like you are frustrated with your daughter's behavior," or "You really would like to be respected by your daughter." Alternatively, they could give a more direct restatement: "You want your daughter to talk to you and not shut you out." Whichever reflection is used, it is important for mediators to signal either verbally or nonverbally that this is a perception and invite the participant to confirm, deny, or clarify the perception. Mediators can pause with a questioning look or ask, "Did I perceive that correctly?" By letting the parties know that these reflections are a search for accurate information about how this problem makes them feel, mediators show respect and concern for the disputants. These statements encourage parties to take responsibility for their feelings and to correct the mediators if the perception is wrong. Other reflecting statements include, "You *seem* to be feeling miserable because John refuses to pay you the debt," or "It *sounds* like you are puzzled by the behavior of your boss at the staff meeting."

Sometimes it is helpful to practice adding "emotion" words to a listener's vocabulary to be prepared for this active listening. By increasing the number of words that describe feeling, we can help ourselves and others more correctly identify emotions and what lies behind them.

EXERCISE
"Reflecting Feelings"

In dyads, one person picks a word (privately) from the following list and tells of an instance that evoked that feeling. The other person responds by looking at the list and reflecting the feeling. Start out the reflections with statements like:

- "It sounds like you're feeling . . ."
- "I hear your . . ."
- "You are feeling . . ."

After each reflection, the listener needs to check that the identified feeling is the correct one by pausing and waiting for a clarification or asking, "Have I described your feelings correctly?"

angry	enthusiastic
bitter	excited
bored	fearful
comfortable	frustrated
concerned	grateful
content	helpless
devastated	high
disgusted	hopeful
disturbed	humiliated
embarrassed	hurt
empty	inhibited

intimidated	surprised
irritable	suspicious
lukewarm	tense
miserable	terrified
mixed up	trapped
nervous	uneasy
puzzled	vulnerable
resentful	weak
sad	worried
shaky	

Journal Entry

Venting is something I do very well. I love to talk. In conflict, I always assumed that if I was doing all of the talking, then I must be winning. Nothing could be further from the truth. All I was doing by not letting the other person speak was drowning out other opinions. All that achieved was to harden or worsen perceptions of me as a bully—I wasn't "winning," I was losing all opportunity to improve the situation and creating more obstacles to be overcome.

Acknowledging

Throughout the whole mediation process, the mediators can validate or encourage the parties by commending their efforts or confirming that what was said was heard. A common place for acknowledgement is at the beginning of each session—acknowledging their effort in coming to mediation: "Thank you for taking the time and effort to engage in the mediation process." When progress or movement is noted, a mediator can say, "Dispute resolution is hard

work . . . you're doing great!" After particularly
intense emotions, an acknowledgement could be, "I
understand how difficult this must be for you . . .
you're doing fine." As the process is nearing
resolution, mediators can say, "You've both worked so
hard! We are almost ready to write an agreement."

Mediators can continue to use certain phrases and
a positive tone of voice to encourage the parties to
keep talking. For example, phrases like "That is
interesting" and "Yes, I see" help move the process
along and also model effective listening skills.
Listeners who acknowledge the speaker's message
convey their own message of encouragement and
respect.

Problem-Solving Stage

Throughout the introduction and the story-telling
stage, the parties have explained their positions, and
the mediators have begun to clarify the problem by
identifying the issues and interests offered by the
parties. In the problem-solving stage, the problem will
be clearly defined; this step is crucial to the mediation
process. Often, the issues are presented as positions,
sounding like demands or solutions. Mediators can
help to sort out the issues so that each party's interests
can be explored, moving the parties away from
positions. Next, an agenda will be set, and options will
be generated and evaluated.

Defining the Problem

As mediators help disputants to define the
problem, they are identifying essential interests and

moving toward solutions that address them. Positions are often presented as "bottom lines." It is sometimes difficult to see how the two incompatible positions initially presented can ever be reconciled. People negotiating over positions often reach an impasse. Mediators must help participants discover the interests underlying those positions. Interests are the human needs, values, and concerns people hold. If a conflict is to be resolved in a fair and mutually acceptable way, interests must be negotiated. Because interests are usually broader and more negotiable than positions, a creative, win/win solution can result. (Remember our earlier example of the orange.)

Issues in a conflict are the topics that the parties see as the base of the conflict. Issues can focus on: content (facts, money, contracts) or procedures (method of payment, dispute resolution process, time constraints, settlement obstacles). In a family mediation, for example, a mother and a teenage son are discussing a proposed curfew. The position of the mother is that she wants her son home at 10:00 every night. The son's position is that he thinks the curfew is too early, and he wants to stay out until midnight. A search for interests in this situation may reveal the mother's interest in her son's safety, her own fear about being home alone at night, and maybe even fear of losing control of her son. The son may be interested in retaining independence or maintaining a reputation. Issues may emerge concerning content (what the son does from 10 to 12 p.m., why the mother is so afraid) or as procedural (the son is not willing to explore options; the mother has to get back to work soon; or the father is a necessary third party to help them to complete agreements).

As the issues and interests are being identified, mediators need to help the parties see the delineation and the connections. Use of a flip chart, blackboard, or paper to record the lists gives people a better picture of all the motivating factors beneath their positions. The following techniques assist mediators in making the transition from positions to interests:

- Focus on interests vs. positions—Ask "Why does that concern you?"
- Go beyond positions—Ask "What makes that position satisfactory to you?"
- Avoid focusing on or asking about preferred outcomes too early in the process.
- Identify and emphasize common interests and mutual gains—"I am hearing you both state that the safety of the children is a primary concern."
- Generate and promote creative and multiple options in order to obtain a fair solution for all.
- Guiding principle: separate the people from the problem.

EXERCISE
"Positions and Interests"

For each of the three issues in conflict, list and discuss the following:
1. The position of Chris
    The position of Pat
2. Two interests of Chris
    Two interests of Pat
3. Reframe the issue to include both of their interests.

Issues:
  a) Pat and Chris are in the library, disagreeing about whether a window nearby should be open or closed.
  b) Pat and Chris are discussing distribution of household chores in their home. They are in disagreement over who needs to take the trash out on Wednesdays.
  c) Pat is a teacher and wants Chris transferred out of the classroom. They disagree about the transfer.

Agenda Setting

After the issues and interests are clearly identified, mediators are ready to set an agenda, or prioritize concerns before exploring the options. (If there is only one issue in the dispute, participants can move ahead to the option-generating step.) With a multi-issue dispute the parties can state their preference about which issue to discuss first, and they can negotiate a starting point. Mediators sometimes suggest starting with an issue that is nearing resolution or has common interests. By beginning with an easy issue, a conciliatory mood can be set and the parties can experience trust in the process.

On the other hand, participants can choose to start with the most important issue, especially if it seems to be overriding all else. Whichever order is chosen, mediators need to check with both parties to see if they are in agreement. The agenda should be written on a flip chart, blackboard, or paper. The agenda should address whether one meeting is sufficient. If more than one meeting is required, the agenda can

target how much should be accomplished in each
meeting. This may be a good time to discuss time
constraints with the participants so that schedules can
be coordinated and the proper amount of time allotted
to address complex issues conveniently for all parties.

Words of the Wise

*In most people's minds, inventing simply is not
part of the negotiating process. People see their
job as narrowing the gap between positions,
not broadening the options available. They
tend to think, "We're having a hard enough
time agreeing as it is. The last thing we need is
a bunch of different ideas." By looking from
the outset for the single best answer, you are
likely to short circuit a wiser decision-making
process in which you select from a large
number of possible answers.*

Roger Fisher & William Ury (p. 61)

Journal Entry

Creative options would be an excellent way to
start thinking at the grade school level. Maybe
we might have a chance of stopping the
noneffective ways we find everyday answers.

Option Generation

With an agenda in sight, and a clear picture of
each party's interests, mediators can guide the parties
in exploring options. This step in the problem-solving
stage can be powerful if separated into three parts:

review interests, brainstorm options, and evaluate options.

Mediators begin this stage by focusing again on the interests that have been expressed in previous stages. Allow time to review once more what each party needs from an agreement BEFORE looking for solutions. Concerning the issue at hand, a mediator can say, "I see that John needs _____ and Manuel needs_____. If we are able to achieve a solution that meets those interests, would you be satisfied?" Although there is a chance this may lead to more interest exploration, it is helpful to check once more for a clear picture of the interests before moving on.

The second part of option generation is the brainstorming step. This can be initiated by a simple question to each participant, "How do we resolve this?" or one that directly addresses the issue, "What does it mean to be a good neighbor?" Mediators can more formally invite the parties to brainstorm: "I'd like each of you (or both of you together) to brainstorm a list of possible solutions to this problem. Let's be very creative here with all ideas welcomed. Please hold your comments on the options until later when we will evaluate each one. Remember, these are **possible** ideas, not offers that you will be held to." Separating the generating of options from the evaluating of options is a powerful tool that can prevent premature judging that inhibits brainstorming. The mediator should write down each idea with equal verbal and nonverbal gestures. If verbal comments are made, they should also treat each suggestion equally.

At this point, mediators may bring up an offer or solution that was introduced by the disputants earlier in the mediation. These need to be reframed to reflect the interests the parties have identified: "If I remember correctly, you mentioned earlier that you were interested in safety in your neighborhood and suggested_____."

Role-reversal is a mediation technique that stretches the parties' creativity. Invite one party to suggest a solution that would meet the other's needs and vice versa: "Manuel, if you were a car-repair business owner like John, what would you do to ensure customer safety in the parking lot?"

The brainstorming step expands possibilities for resolution, or "expands the pie." With no judgements or evaluations yet, participants feel comfortable to think beyond positions and explore how interests can be met.

EXERCISE
"Connect the Dots"

Make sixteen (16) dots on a piece of paper—four groups of four in a square. Using four connecting lines, cover each dot. Try every possible solution.

The last part of the option generation step is to evaluate the options. Mediators call this "reality testing" or "reality checking." Mediators use the interest list generated as the objective criteria for judging the efficacy of the solutions suggested. Questions are asked to make sure each option is one parties can live with. The goal is to determine if the options are fair, clear, and realistic. Mediators should probe perceptions of the parties—remembering that fairness and clearness are from the disputants' perceptions, not the mediator's! When checking if the option is realistic, mediators can ask questions like, "If this option were put into place, how would it work?" "Will this option meet both of your needs?" "How will this solution affect you?" "Can you afford these payments?" "Will this schedule fit your work day?"

At this stage, both the mediators and the parties are anxious to be done. Mediators may need to slow things down to assure a lasting and workable agreement. Considering long- and short-term implications helps test the option: "This sounds good to you today; will it work for you a year from now?" If it seems that one of the parties has caved in or given up, mediators can carefully check with them: "Earlier you stated that you would never agree to pay $500; I'm wondering what has changed now?"

If, after a thorough evaluation of all options, the parties feel there are no options on which they can agree, they can take some comfort in the knowledge that they have thoroughly explored all possibilities. Parties should be commended on the hard work of brainstorming and evaluating options. They should have a much better picture of each other's interests, and that picture can impact their future relationship even without a mediated agreement. This picture can be an acceptable resolution to them.

When parties reach a mutually acceptable resolution, the mediation process can seem like "magic." Pearce and Littlejohn (in press) note that the magic is sometimes missed, and parties cannot reach agreement. If the parties hold differing expectations of what mediation should be, they can be conversing, bargaining, and negotiating from entirely different perspectives without moving toward agreement.

Pearce and Littlejohn tell the story of one student, Margaret, who took her jacket to a tailor, Park, to have the sleeves shortened. Margaret came to mediation wanting reimbursement for the jacket because Park had cut the sleeves too short. Park, a Korean interested in "good-faith" offers and harmonious relationships, made an offer that Margaret haughtily refused. Park saw the mediators as arbitrators who would judge the quality of his workmanship; Margaret saw mediation as a way to get money. Pearce and Littlejohn wrote, "no matter how much they tried to explain mediation, Park, who had limited ability in English, did not seem to understand. We think the misunderstanding was more than linguistic; it was cultural as well." (pp. 5–14)

Journal Entry

In mediation and negotiation, agreements for the sake of agreement tend to lead to disappointment. It is important that disputants be clear about what their interests are and be persistent in seeing that the agreement is one which they can support.

Resolution Stage

The option exploration process should reveal, at a minimum, commonalities and ideally some compatible options. Mediators are now ready to help parties form an agreement that is satisfactory to them both. More questions start the agreement writing stage: "Now that you've agreed on these two options, how do we make a resolution incorporating them?" Make sure that all the points both parties feel are important are included in the agreement. The agreement needs to have balance, with suggestions for resolution coming from each of the participants.

Most agreement forms have spaces for dates, names of all parties, signatures, and lines to write the agreement. Some mediators write the agreement on a separate sheet of paper and type up the agreement later to be sent to both sides. Other mediators write the agreements at the table, using the disputants' own words. Whichever method of agreement writing is chosen, it is important to make sure the parties are agreeing to what is being written. Further reality testing can go on here, checking if the terms are workable and actually solve the problem. Make sure the most minute details are written down, not leaving any room for disagreements: "Who is going to pay for the fence?" "How high will the fence be?" "What color will the fence be painted?"

Before the final signatures are given, mediators need to offer a last opportunity to ask questions or make comments. This is another place to watch for nonverbal signals of discomfort from the parties. Displays of continued anger or resentment may signal discomfort with the agreement. Behaviors such as head in hands or staring at the wall could mean parties are resigned to an agreement they don't want. Tears, fidgeting, or other signs of nervousness may need to be clarified with careful questions. Although it would be hard to discontinue writing the agreement at this point, it is better to end the mediation than to have the parties agree to something with which they are not happy.

Other reasons for not writing an agreement may include:

1. hesitancy to put agreements in writing, not trusting confidentiality
2. parties need more information; they want to postpone a final agreement until after talking with a boss, a spouse, etc.
3. strong entrenchment in positions, unable to move toward interest-based negotiating
4. preference to settle matter in court

Even the best-intentioned people sometimes cannot or do not reach a win/win solution. After all, there are some pies that have a limited number of pieces (number of children, amount of money, time available). The desire to learn what the other person wants and the effort to satisfy those desires can build a climate of collaboration that can do some preventive work for the future of their relationship. Mediators need to remember that they are there to manage the process, not save relationships or heal an unhealthy business deal. By participating in the mediation process and observing the skills modelled by the mediator, people learn to assess their interests and to see how to participate in interest-based negotiations.

Journal Entry

One party plainly refused to sign anything, no matter what was written or agreed upon. This sense of stubbornness and paranoia was impossible for me to work around and still remain neutral.

Closure

The final minutes of the mediation process will include handing out copies of the agreement, handshakes, and some last commendations for choosing a process that allows the parties to participate in managing their own disputes. It is important to remain "in neutral" until the parties have left the room. Sometimes, a disputant will remain after the mediation in an attempt to discuss the case with the mediators. Mediators need to remain impartial, stating they were there as process managers with no interest in the terms or content.

Often after a session, mediators feel it is helpful to "debrief" with other mediators concerning the session. This is a time for discussion of the ups and downs of the process, including evaluation and suggestions that would have helped the process move smoother. Conflict situations can be emotional and stressful, and this informal time can relieve stress for the mediators and prepare them better for next time.

Journal Entry

My first real mediation! All of the stuff actually works when put to the test. Every place I came to an impasse, I remembered another idea we had from role plays or scenarios. I found that role reversals really worked well. There was a lot of tension between the parties because they knew they would have to face each other at work after the session.

Chapter 4

Special Concerns

Mediation is still in the early stages of establishing its place alongside our current adversarial systems, the legal system in particular. The emergence of mediation has been called a "muffled explosion" as it tries to work out the kinks that accompany any new behavior. Scholars in the disciplines of communication, law, sociology, political science, and many others are researching the dilemmas and considerations that accompany this collaborative dispute-resolution process. This chapter will explore five critical issues for the mediation process: appropriateness (intake concerns), the use of a caucus, the co-mediator model, cultural considerations, and ethics.

Appropriateness

People often express doubts about how well a process like mediation will work. Adler and Towne (1990) see three questions that arise when confronted with win/win negotiating. First, people ask the question, "Isn't the win/win approach too good to be true?" (p. 388). It is evident that there are some disputes where a win/lose outcome is the only one available. When there is only one car to be awarded in a divorce agreement, they both cannot have the car.

When there are two office spaces for three people, one person will get the private space and two will have to share. Most of the time, with mediation, the creativity and good intentions of the participants lead to satisfying outcomes.

A second question that arises is "Is it possible to change others?" (p. 392). In attempting mediation, one often hears, "This process looks great to me, but it will be impossible to get my partner to cooperate." If mediators model the collaborative communication skills described above from the first interaction with disputants (whether on the phone or in person), these behaviors may be adopted by the disputants when they get together to work on the problem. Respect and sincerity can inspire similar behavior. Mediators can also encourage parties by showing that the costs of competing are severe, while the benefits of collaborating are rewarding. By showing that it is in the parties' best interests to work together, the mediator can help disputants move beyond animosity to a postion where cooperation is possible.

A third common question is, "Isn't win/win negotiating **too** rational?" (p. 392). Many disputants feel that they are just too emotional or worked up to go through the mediation process successfully. It is important to remember not just to reflect feelings, but to reflect the *intensity* of the feelings. As stated earlier, the emotional part of the conflict needs a necessary emotion-venting period before the rational, content-related issues can be explored. Mediators can use statements like, "You are extremely angry today. It looks like you need to tell us about your anger," "I can see the intensity of your frustration, and we will work today to understand what brought you to this point," or "It must be extremely difficult to consider negotiating when you are so broken-hearted. Let's slow down and learn about your sadness."

Journal Entry

Because we live in a realistic versus idealistic society, there is a need for other forms of conflict resolution besides mediation. This fact is important to remember if one is to practice any of these techniques with living, breathing subjects. Sometimes a fresh approach may work better in a situation where an agreement seems unobtainable. It is the individual responsibility of all professionals who act as conflict resolvers to recognize the point where their efforts are not helping the parties involved.

Collaborative solutions are possible when parties possess the proper attitude and skills. If individuals have a positive motivation concerning the mediation process, they will be more likely to listen to each other and attempt to understand. Parties who do not want to resolve their problems or are stuck in their positions may not want to use mediation for their dispute. If it is apparent that another form of intervention is needed, the voluntary nature of mediation needs to be upheld, and referrals can be given to the appropriate agency. Although the decision to mediate usually rests with the parties, mediators and intake workers can assist in that effort. The following questions can help with the decision:

- Is each party there voluntarily? Individuals forced into mediation may not be participating in "good faith."
- Can the parties communicate and *hear* each other? Is the emotional component of the parties so strong that the parties cannot see past it?
- Are the parties able to identify and express issues and interests for themselves?
- Is each party open to reaching a result that is fair to the other?

When a case is being considered for mediation, there is usually an intake person or intake staff to record some preliminary information, such as general demographics and a short description of the conflict, how long it has been occurring, who are the other parties involved, and who needs to be present to have authority to settle.

When mediators are selected for a case, intake staff assure that mediators can hear the issues without bias. Mediators can be biased concerning issues about which they have strong opinions, values, and morals. Mediators may also have some type of affiliation with one or more of the parties. If either of these biases occurs, the mediator has a responsibility to disclose the possible presentiment to the parties or disqualify himself/herself.

The intake staff assesses factors such as willingness to use a collaborative process, communication competency, tendencies toward extreme anger or violence, or the necessity of the case being handled by a more appropriate agency (as in the case of a rights or policy violation). If both parties are willing to come to the table and attempt to reach a mutually satisfactory agreement, and characteristics that would hinder the process—such as those discussed above—are not evident, the case should be considered a candidate for the mediation process. Intake workers should *not* prejudge whether or not this case will be successful.

Caucus

The caucus, as described earlier, is a break in the mediation process. Mediators meet individually with each disputant for an equal amount of time. Information disclosed in a caucus can remain confidential or can be disclosed when the parties reunite, depending on the wishes of the parties stated in caucus. **Remember**, ask each party at the end of their caucus session if they would like the content of the caucus confidential or if it can be shared with the other party. There are times when a caucus can be helpful and can be considered:

- The mediation has reached an impasse because of rigid positions.
- Mediators suspect there is some hidden agenda or information needed that the parties are unwilling to bring out.
- Emotions are high and it is evident the parties need a break from each other.
- Issues that are being avoided in a joint session can be clarified in a caucus.
- One or both of the disputants seem to need encouragement.
- Mediators have lost control of the session.
- One or both parties would need to take a risk to move further toward agreement.

The use of caucuses vary widely among mediators. Although the benefits can be numerous, there are also some cautions involved. Because of the importance of knowing how to use a caucus successfully and integrating the information gained in the caucus into the full session, inexperienced or not-so-confident mediators may not want to use a caucus. Some disadvantages of a caucus include:

- Time spent with individual disputants may appear biased.
- Caucuses dilute one of the strengths of mediation—face-to-face dialogue.
- Material shared is requested to remain confidential; the material may be necessary for agreement.
- The flow and equilibrium of the session may be disturbed.
- In a co-mediator model, both mediators may not agree on the use of a caucus.

If the mediator decides a caucus session is appropriate, it is important to keep the time balanced and brief. If a long time passes, the disputant waiting outside may get suspicious or nervous. The same communication skills used throughout the whole session need to be used in a caucus. Venting of emotions is encouraged, content is reframed and restated, and acknowledgement of progress should be noted. This separate meeting can produce more flexibility and creativity if used appropriately.

Co-Mediator Model

The use of two mediators working together to facilitate the dispute resolution process is common. In community mediation programs, divorce and family mediation, and many court-connected programs, co-mediation has many advantages. If cases are particularly complex, it is helpful to have two mediators to untangle the issues. In programs where there are a large number of mediators, particularly when there are apprentice or inexperienced mediators, co-mediation benefits all parties involved. Novice mediators benefit from the experience and from participation with someone who has handled a number of situations. Participants benefit from having one more set of eyes and ears to offer perceptions. The following are advantages of co-mediation:

- The combined communication skills add to the effectiveness of the process.
- Two mediators can better mirror the ethnicity, gender, age, class, and any other considerations a program may be meeting.
- In multi-issue or multi-party cases, the tension or stress can be reduced with two mediators to diffuse tensions.
- Mediators can have substantive expertise that can complement each other (process skills, family matters, legal considerations, empathy, workplace knowledge, etc.).
- Mediator bias is lessened with two mediators, encouraging the greater possibility of trust by disputants in at least one of the mediators.

There are some possible disadvantages to using a co-mediator model:

- For the program, there is an increased complexity of scheduling, costs increase, and need for a number of mediators increases.

- Two mediators can increase the cost for the parties.
- The two mediators may have incompatible styles.

As the mediation field emerges, mediator styles and methods of practice are diverging. Deborah Kolb (1994) explores the diversity in mediation styles by investigating the different social fields in which mediation occurs. Looking at mediators from arenas as diverse as public policy, divorce, court proceedings, labor grievances, profit-making, neighborhood justice centers, and international areas, Kolb notes the struggle in this evolving profession of mediation. Mediators may work with individual or interpersonal disputes or may involve groups or organizations.

Most mediation programs encourage use of a co-mediator team with similar styles and experiences for conducting mediations. Often the mediators are trained within the program and move up through the ranks as apprentices to another mediator who serves as a mentor.

The growth of mediation programs in communities, courts, schools, and workplaces has increased the demand for skilled mediators. Inexperienced mediators need opportunities to gain practice. The co-mediator model provides an excellent opportunity, as mentioned above. There is no substitute for participating in managing actual conflicts. With proper training in communication skills and mediation techniques, novice mediators can continue learning in real-life situations while also contributing to solving problems. Co-mediation is an excellent illustration of the win/win situation we have been describing. The following discussion of culture points to the need for mediators who can mirror disputants from varied backgrounds.

Cultural Considerations

Diversity is a topic that has everyone's attention. The United States is home to a multitude of cultures. Since culture encompasses all the behaviors we have learned—values, customs, morals, language, laws, education, family, communication and any other capability—it has a profound and often subconscious effect on all interactions. Paul Bohannan (1992, p. 13) refers to culture as "a means of standardizing choices and of sharing successful results of choices made by others in the past." Mediators must learn about the varying cultures and the social expectations they may encounter. Some mediators feel the need to study a culture carefully before attempting a mediation with people from that group; others see that due to time constraints it is difficult to have a clear picture of the culture under consideration. Sunoo (1990) offers some observations and suggestions that can be helpful when considering conduct for cross-cultural mediation.

1. **Expect different expectations**.

   Differing expectations are brought to the bargaining table when individuals from different cultures confront each other. Responses are often misinterpreted, and otherwise assumed "rules of the game" cannot be taken for granted. Some cultures may see elderly persons as wise and deserving of respect, while others may have a different perception, placing 30- to 40-year-old academics at the top of the wisdom scale.

2. **Do not assume that what you say is being understood**.

The same words spoken in English often have different meanings and emphasis to people from different cultures. In his experience mediating with differing cultures, former President Jimmy Carter (1993) believes it is important to create a framework for discussion by making sure there is shared meaning for words. For example, Carter saw that for one participant in a mediation, to "mediate" was to "dominate"; "compromise" meant "total surrender"; and an "observer" was an "active negotiator."

3. **Listen carefully.**
Be ready to apply your active listening skills and to reinterpret what you perceive vis-à-vis the cultural orientation of the participants. Determine what concerns and interests each party is trying to communicate with his or her proposal. It takes planning, commitment, and practice to listen actively. This listening includes paying attention to both the verbals and nonverbals of the disputant. For example, different cultures regard silence in different ways. A Native American disputant can indicate agreement by silence (respect for the decision), while to another this silence could be seen as indecision or hesitancy. Westerners are often uncomfortable or awkward with silences in conversation or, more specifically, in mediation. They see silence as a negative action, one that signifies lack of interest, boredom, or confusion. Asian and Native American cultures see silence as a sign of respect. A talkative person can be seen as a show-off or as an insincere person. Mediators need to be aware of the use of silence, noting the

disputants' comfort or discomfort and adjusting accordingly.

4. **Seek ways of getting both parties to validate the concerns of the other.**
For example, a mediator might say, "Margaret, can I ask you to help us see your understanding of Park's interest in harmonious relationships?" The mediator then asks Park to do the same thing concerning Margaret's need for fair compensation for the tailored-too-short jacket sleeves. Role reversals are most effective in sharing perspectives. Mediators might ask, "Margaret, if you were a tailor wanting to promote good faith and recognition of your skilled tailoring, what would you offer to a customer dissatisfied with service?" Always make sure to have both parties participate in the role reversal.

5. **Be patient, be humble, and be willing to learn.**
Americans often expect instant gratification, instant results, instant responses. Many people from other cultures work on a different, often more slowly paced timetable. Impatience is viewed in many cultures as a sign of immaturity rather than enthusiasm; loud displays of confidence may be interpreted as arrogance; and insistence on the rules of the game may be seen as disrespect for how others have learned to interact. In a separate caucus, take time to point out that potential differences could stem from cultural differences, and encourage each party to accept and learn something from the other.

6. **Apply "win/win" negotiating principles to the negotiation rather than traditional adversarial bargaining techniques.**

Define issues rather than taking hard initial positions. Discuss interests and concerns of both sides. Try to come up with multiple options for solving the problems of both parties. Apply fair standards to select the options, and work through a consensus process to arrive at solutions rather than using power plays. In the Margaret and Park example, if mediators saw common interests emerge, such as "reputation" or "pride," they could remark, "Let's begin a search for options that could fulfill Margaret's interest in pride in professional clothing and Park's interest in pride in workmanship. Margaret, let's start with you. Can you think of an option that could serve the reputation of both of you?"

7. **Dare to do things differently.**
   Throughout the world, there are literally thousands of legitimate and different ways for two parties to reach an agreement. Just because **we** feel comfortable with one set of rules and etiquette does not mean that it is necessarily the most logical, efficient, or desirable method for everyone.
   Cross-cultural differences are not necessarily only ethnic-based. Mediators need to see many other characteristics of people that surface in mediation. Besides ethnic differences, there are age, gender, political, socioeconomic, sexual orientation, workplace experience and background, and religious differences. When people from different cultures conflict, they often try to impose their own culture on the other party. A skilled mediator will guide the negotiation so it is concerned with the issue and not with cultural differences.

EXERCISE
"Looking at Culture"

Look through a newspaper and list the cultural issues that could or do create conflict. Identify the values that created the differences. Try to discover an underlying interest or goal that could be compatible. Share one or two examples with the class or small group.

When parties reach a point in a mediation where cultural, gender, economic, or age differences create an impasse or at least demand attention, mediators can use communication skills to neutralize the situation. Restatements and summaries that remove the focus on stereotypical behavior help create a neutral atmosphere:

- "Her family is so tight-fisted, they selfishly save every penny."
  "You really seem concerned with different approaches to saving or spending money."
- "John is such a pig! He never takes his eyes off my breasts when talking to me."
  "Sounds like you are uncomfortable with the way John stares at you when he talks."
- "My boss expects me to tell 'a little lie' to the contractor. How dare she insult me that way!"
  "You are not comfortable lying."
- "How can I get any sleep with those disrespectful, drunk, and hateful teenagers next door?"
  "I see that the behavior of your neighbors disturbs you."

By attempting to take the emphasis off the accusations or judgements of differences, mediators can continue to explore issues while avoiding confrontation.

EXERCISE
"Neutralizing Cultural Accusations"

For the following remarks in a mediation, reframe the statement to make it more neutral.

- "She couldn't possibly understand; she lives in that minority neighborhood on the west side."
- "Those poor people bring our property values down."
- "He chooses the gay lifestyle just to get attention."
- "Abortion is a sin."
- "My boss can't run this office; she's too busy balancing her checkbook."
- "How can he expect anyone from Mexico to run this computer?"
- "I'm the oldest person here, so I should get priority."

Particular challenges for mediators arise when differences are deeper or less obvious than surface issues and are actually conflicting perceptions of reality. Littlejohn, Shailor, and Pearce (1994) believe that when differences involve incompatible conceptions of morality, justice, and conflict, it is like "one person trying to play chess and another person checkers on the same board" (p. 68). The mediators also come into the situation with their own view of reality, so there exist many differences here to coordinate or match if possible.

To manage these deep differences, Littlejohn et al. (1994) see three paths that may assist in the mediation. The mediators can try to achieve common ground among the various realities: 1) The parties can be encouraged to accept the realities of the mediators' process. 2) The mediators can assimilate to the disputants' realities—a solution usually not desirable from the standpoint of a mediation program with rules and guidelines that are difficult to bend. 3) Individual attention can be given to each disputant, helping him/her to understand issues from the other disputant's viewpoint. This option may mean that the mediators reframe issues differently for each disputant, based on differing perceptions of reality. In other words, mediators must be skilled in basic intercultural communication skills. They may need to step outside of their attempts to discover win/win solutions (collaboration) from time to time and not expect disputants to conform to the mediation process expectations. To suggest this manner of dealing with deep differences in the views of realities of disputants, Littlejohn, et al. find that "the practice of mediation can take on very different meanings as they [mediators] interface with the social realities of various disputants" (p. 82). The challenges created by cultural and other differences add to the responsibility of mediators.

Words of the Wise

Transformation happens only through the process of interaction; it cannot occur in isolation. When, for example, you see your position as the only right or correct one and are not willing to consider or to try to understand other positions, transformation is not possible. Neither can it occur when one perspective is privileged over others. Transformation is generated when you share your perspective with others—when it is subject to comparison with other perspectives in a process of discovery, questioning, and rethinking.

Sonja K. Foss & Karen A. Foss (p. 4)

Ethics

Professional organizations for mediators have been developing model ethical codes for mediators for two decades. Codes have been developed within organizations, communities, states, and schools. Some codes are designed especially for family mediators concerned with parent-child or domestic issues, or attorney mediators attending to court-connected cases. This book recognizes and reflects national standards on ethical development, particularly the *Ethical Standards of Professional Responsibility* of the Society for Professionals in Dispute Resolution, and the *Mediator Code of Ethics* adopted by the Mediation Alliance.

It is the mediator's ethical responsibility to:

- *Be impartial.* A mediator should be free of favoritism or bias in appearance, word, or action. Mediators have a duty to disclose any *conflict of interest*, which would hinder their neutrality regarding the disputants or the dispute.
- *Maintain confidentiality.* The mediators will inform the parties of the extent to which the content of the mediation will be kept confi-

dential and will maintain that confidentiality except in cases of suspected or admitted child abuse or threat of bodily harm to self or others.

- *Informed consent.* Mediators will ensure that the parties are coming to mediation voluntarily, understanding the process and the mediator's role.
- *Disclosure of fees.* Mediators will ensure that the parties understand the costs and the basis of fees at the outset.
- *Full opportunity to express interests.* Mediators ensure that the parties have opportunity for full expression and will empower the parties to be responsible for their own resolution.
- *Suspension/termination/withdrawal.* If participants are unable or unwilling to participate effectively, mediators can terminate the mediation when it is appropriate to do so. Parties should be informed that they have the right to terminate the process when they feel it is appropriate.
- *Legal issues.* Mediators should not give legal advice. A mediator shall not knowingly participate in an illegal agreement. Lawyers for the parties shall not be excluded if the parties want them present.
- Mediators have a responsibility to improve and maintain their professional skills.

These ethical considerations emphasize that mediators have a duty to the parties, to the profession, and to themselves. Because mediation is a profession with ethical responsibilities, it is recommended that those who engage in the practice of mediation follow this code.

Chapter 5

Face Issues

Let us now turn from others to the point of view of the individual who presents himself before them. He may wish them to think highly of him, or to think that he thinks highly of them, or to perceive how in fact he feels toward them, or to obtain no clear-cut impression; he may wish to ensure sufficient harmony so that the interaction can be sustained, or to defraud, get rid of, confuse, mislead, antagonize, or insult them.

Erving Goffman (p. 3)

In Japan, there are words to describe the often incompatible presentation we make of our public versus our private selves. *Tatemae* is the "outside face" one presents publicly; *honne* is the "inner face," which is one's private—often more honest—thoughts.

Individuals who enter a conflict management situation will be dealing with a variety of "face" issues. People often have an image of themselves that they wish to maintain in their interactions. When confronted with a conflict situation, a person's identity, or face, can be made vulnerable or threatened. If face issues are not dealt with, the conflict stagnates there, and the original issues are never addressed. For example, in a divorce and child custody mediation, the couple could find themselves discussing or arguing about "who is the better parent" instead of which parent will have the children for Christmas. In understanding the different aspects of face issues, it is helpful to look at **types of face needs**, and **how mediators can deal with face issues.**

Types of Face Needs

S. R. Wilson and Linda Putnam (1990, pp. 374–406) see four different kinds of face needs that motivate people to pursue their goals. Individuals can either maintain, save, attack, or support face. When trying to preserve one's image as a respected, competent, and trustworthy person, one is **maintaining** face. A car salesman can maintain face by stating the number of happy customers he or she has had. A therapist can give a long presentation on how she or he is dedicated to preserving the confidentiality of clients. A teenage boy can tell stories of how he was the first one done building a table in shop class. By bolstering positive personal attributes, individuals can maintain face and protect themselves from possible attack in those areas.

It can become necessary to **save** face when it has been damaged or attacked. These "attacks" could be real or imagined, yet people need to repair this damaged image in some way. One can save face by shifting attention away from the attack, changing the subject, minimizing the issue, or joking about it. Face-saving is also accomplished by denying the attack or rejecting it ("I didn't inhale" "I have never lied on my income tax"). Persons can save face by putting themselves in a more defensible position by changing their story or making the issue foggy ("What I really meant to say is . . ." "Whether that is true or not, this is the most important point"). These are defensive moves that enable people to repair an image they are concerned with keeping.

People can also attempt to deal with face-saving needs by **attacking** the other's face. By making the other person seem distrustful or unworthy of respect, individuals feel they are portraying themselves as more respectful or trustworthy. This tactic is most evident in advertising campaigns where companies attack the credibility of the competitor's product to make theirs look better. In the world of politics, attacks on the opposing candidate are an effort to bolster the face of the attacker. Such situations can easily get out of control and lose focus on actual issues.

When parties **support** the face of the other, they are meeting the face needs of the other to accomplish the goals at hand. The face-supporting tactics often reduce the other's need to attack, even if the two parties still disagree on the issues at hand. In a divorce mediation, a parent can support the other's face by noting "You are great with the children" or "You have consistently shown up on time for our meetings."

Two large-scale negotiations in 1994 offered contrasting approaches to face issues. In the baseball strike in 1994, the players and the owners remained at a stand-off for months, eventually having to cancel the remainder of the season and the world series. In this author's research, there were no offers of face-support from either side. In the global controversy concerning removal of dictator Cedras from Haiti in 1994, ex-president Jimmy Carter offered Cedras many face-supporting statements, telling him in essence that Carter was interested in Cedras' motivations, his desires for his country, and his plans for the future. That negotiation had some positive results and reduced the need for Cedras to attack Carter personally. Face-supporting skills can be used by mediators or by individuals in negotiation to ensure a smoother and more successful process.

EXERCISE
"Face-Needs Identification"

In the transcript below, find the face needs. Identify if the employer and/or the employee are maintaining, saving, attacking, or supporting.

Employer:
1. I spend almost all of my time supervising you people!
2. The report will not be ready on time because I had more important things to do.
3. I am happy to have an employee like you who arrives at these meetings on time.
4. Did you notice that I completed the last three reports on time?
5. If only we had competent secretaries like the people in the office down the hall.

Employee:
1. It is miserable working with a dictator like you.
2. I spend all my time trying to decipher your writing.

3. Of course I didn't type up the memo; I thought that was Mary's job.
4. I have arrived at every staff meeting on time.
5. It is so encouraging to us employees when you provide these donuts and coffee.
6. I have never made a mistake on a budget projection yet!

Face Issues in Mediation

When face issues are not addressed in conflict situations, destructive cycles can occur with either escalating face attacks or competing attempts at face maintenance. These cycles can impede a dispute resolution process either because the parties regress to a discussion centered around face issues instead of the real issues, or because one party "caves in" if unsuccessful at saving face. Wilson (1992) notes that third-party interventions can break such cycles by reducing the threat to face and modeling a more flexible and creative process that does not entail the face competitiveness.

With the communication skills discussed earlier in this text, mediators have the tools to allow disputants to maintain face. Mediators who use active listening techniques that reframe an issue or reflect inflammatory remarks into neutral language can redirect attention to the issue by taking words that have the potential to attack face out of the statement. A comment such as "She's such a liar; how can I believe that the check will arrive on time?" can be reframed by the mediator: "So you are concerned with receiving your payment on time." This reframed statement takes out the face-attack ("liar") and puts the focus on the issue to be dealt with according to the goal of resolving the conflict. If the issue is an interpersonal one concerning a habitual liar, the statement can still be reframed neutrally: "I hear that you are feeling upset by her dishonesty." By reflecting feelings, the mediator takes the emphasis off of the "liar" and onto the "feeler."

When mediators acknowledge and validate the disputants, they are choosing positive statements and initiating movement that can maintain face and sometimes save face while avoiding face attacks. After two hours in mediation, mediators can commend the parties on their one area of agreement instead of despairing over the three areas of impasse. By noting even small successes, participants can feel responsible for the accomplishments and be more likely to examine their role in the dispute. Mediators can support face with statements such as, "This certainly is a highly emotional conflict, and I am pleased at the common interests you've discovered and the one area of agreement. Congratulations!" or "You are each making a great effort to understand each other. John, it seems difficult for you to accept Mary's lifestyle, but you seem to be attempting to see her point of view. Mary, I noticed your distress at the possibility of moving, but you are collaborating with John toward solutions in a positive way." Mediators can note the image participants are seeking to maintain and offer statements to support that image.

A mediator can look for and become aware of the issues that would be a threat to face by participants. By approving and supporting flexibility, the mediator can model what Roxanne Luloffs (1994) calls **conflict competence**. She notes that

> threatening another person's self-image in a conflict puts the focus on restoring the image rather than on dealing with the issue in the conflict. Threats to face are created largely when people lock themselves and others into untenable positions because they equate flexibility with inconsistency. (p. 193)

Mediators can accept the parties' right to change their minds. Compromise later in a negotiation or discarding a bottom line can be seen as "selling out" to some participants. As mentioned earlier, this "selling out" or "caving in" can alert mediators to a need for more reality checking, but it can be acknowledged in a way that saves face. Remarking **neutrally**, about a new position or interest, and noting the difference from an earlier stated interest, mediators signal a flexible process that can include changing one's mind and, thus, creating face maintenance.

Leslie Fagre (1995) sees a mediator as a "face manager" for the parties. When the mediators encourage parties to separate the people from the problem, the focus is taken off of the potentially "failed" relationship. Whether a husband-wife, teacher-student, employer-employee, salesperson-customer, or neighbor-neighbor, the relationship may be entangled by feelings such as jealousy, anger, betrayal or hurt. By dealing with those issues separately and then viewing a shared problem that the parties can resolve together, parties can begin to see their commonalities. Fagre (1995) notes,

From the beginning of the session, mediators
stress group efforts and shared goals of the
process. At different times throughout the
session, mediators may commend the disputants for their hard work and cooperative
spirit and remind them of the progress they
have made together. (p. 3)

Mediator strategies and process goals can be a
valuable aid to parties in conflict. By minimizing
differences and encouraging a search for commonalities, parties can move forward without a fear of
losing face. Substantive conflict can be productive. It
stimulates thought about a specific problem, and both
parties' opinions can be pooled to create a good
solution. Affective conflict, such as face issues, creates
an unsettling atmosphere that frustrates those
involved and diverts their attention from the real
issue. They are much more likely to engage in
avoidance or escalation behaviors than in cooperative
decision making.

EXERCISE
"Neutral Statements"

Change the following face-threatening statements into neutral statements.

1. I hate the way she flirts with every man
    who comes into the office.
2. After three times winning "Employee of
    the Month" you'd think I'd get a little
    respect.
3. How can I trust him to change the dia-
    pers on little Billy when it is needed?

4. I have approached the teacher and nicely asked him to review the test, and he still ignores me.
5. It's difficult to control this wild class when there is one of me and thirty of them.
6. What a sexist pig!

Chapter 6

War and Dance

The use of a collaborative model of dispute resolution signals something broader than "this is a step before you use the more formal processes or go to court." What Alternative Dispute Resolution proponents are saying is that these processes offer choices that differ from the formal processes, a shift in power balancing that gives disputants an interactive role in resolving their disputes, an education concerning a method of dealing with conflict that surpasses positional bargaining, and a forum for looking deeper at underlying interests. Whether seen as the difference between collaboration and adversarial confrontation or between cooperation and competitiveness, individuals are encouraged to note the choice one has when choosing an intervention to help them resolve their dispute. Verderber and Verderber (1992) see one indication of the difference:

> When a conflict arises, the variable that first affects the outcome of the conflict is the participant's level of competitive or cooperative behavior. If the participants are competitive, they are likely to introduce negative means in order to "win" the conflict, and as a result, their egos are likely to be involved. Conversely, if the participants

97

are cooperative, they are willing to follow
the steps of the problem-solving method: (1)
identify the problem, (2) analyze the nature
of the problem, (3) suggest possible solutions, and (4) select the solution that best
meets the needs determined in the problem
analysis. (p. 303)

How can we attend to this variable (compete or
cooperate) when determining the appropriate way to
handle conflict? The answer most likely lies early in
conflicts, when participants first notice that they have
differences and/or that they need a third party's
intervention. We draw from the work of Littlejohn,
Shailor, and Pearce (1994), and from linguists Lakoff
and Johnson (1980).

As mentioned earlier, Littlejohn et al. (1994) point
out that disputants come into conflict with not just
differing goals and interests but with differing social
realities. These researchers defined these realities in
three parts—moral reality (what is proper and right,
one's basic moral assumptions), conflict reality (what
conflict is and how it should be handled), and justice
reality (what is just and fair). An initial perception of
these realities in disputants (particularly the conflict
dimension) can give the mediator a picture of what to
expect in a dispute resolution process. This indication
can be considered—with some caution—during the
intake exploration in alternative dispute resolution
programs.

When considering the variable of "cooperate or
compete," we can be dealing with a conceptual system
in people that governs the way they act, think, and
behave. Lakoff and Johnson (1980) see this system as
language-based and identifiable by the metaphors

used in everyday language. One common metaphor that structures our lives is: "**argument is war**" (p. 4). Note how the following statements use "war" terms: We win and lose arguments, we attack our opponents, we count our wins and losses (time, money, energy, resources), we strategize and build defenses for our positions. Taking the same metaphor and applying it to conflict, we find that many people in conflict situations seem to live in the metaphorical system that "**conflict is war**." Look at the words of Lakoff and Johnson (1980, pp. 4, 5) and insert the word "conflict" for the word "argument."

> Try to imagine a culture where arguments are not viewed in terms of war, where no one wins or loses, where there is no sense of attacking or defending, gaining or losing ground. Imagine a culture where an argument is viewed as a dance, the participants are seen as performers, and the goal is to perform in a balanced and aesthetically pleasing way.

In mediation, participants can take part in a dance, expecting differing degrees of difficulty because of the common metaphorical system "conflict is war" embedded in the Western conscience. Collaborative dispute resolution behaviors allow disputants to experience or view a new metaphorical system. By modelling such an approach, mediators can encourage a mutual desire to handle conflict successfully.

EXERCISE
"Create a Metaphor"

Read the following bridge metaphor and then try to create one of your own concerning conflict, mediation, mediators, or any aspect of the process. You may want to use one of these: circle, fan, meal, cart, community, body, game, physics.

Mediators are like a group of people who build and maintain a bridge over a deep ravine between two villages. The bridge opens avenues of communication between the villages that didn't previously exist. The bridge has to support the weight of any reasonable vehicle driving over it, without denying access to smaller vehicles. It can be used for many purposes—commercial, political, or personal. It can be used as a neutral place to meet as well as a conduit for trade. The maintenance includes ensuring that access is open to both sides and that traffic proceeds in an orderly fashion over the bridge. The builders use guardrails, speed limits, and designated lanes to help ensure the safety of travelers. The builders do all of these things, but they can't force people to use the bridge or to plan their trips across the bridge wisely. They can only hope that they have helped both of the villages to achieve something better in their lives. Their success is not measured by the results of what people do after they have used the bridge, but by the fact that the bridge supported them and provided a way across the ravine.

—Jeff Grant

Journal Entry

I remember hearing that mediation could effect change on the whole of a person's life. I thought, "No way. It's a cool thing, but life changing?" My thinking was wrong. I have never been this enthused about anything I've studied, with the exception of learning to read. It has started to effect changes on my life. My temper doesn't show itself anywhere near as much as it used to. I see more opportunities than I ever had before in my personal life, in school, in my future. Some of these opportunities have appeared in the middle of situations I would have previously seen as nothing more than a depressing drag. I've only begun to scratch the surface of where I think that ADR will take me.

APPENDIX

Agreement to Mediate

1. The mediator is a neutral third party who facilitates a process of dispute management, issue clarification, and option generation. The role of the mediator is to assist the clients in reaching a mutually acceptable plan to manage the issues in dispute.
2. The mediator is not a judge, arbitrator, lawyer, counselor, or advocate in this process. The decision-making power rests with the parties.
3. The mediator does not provide legal services or advice.
4. The parties in the mediation agree not to call the mediator as a witness in any judicial proceedings.
5. Each party agrees to make a sincere effort to resolve the dispute.
6. A mediation will be terminated under the following circumstances:
    *   The parties reach a mutually acceptable agreement.
    *   The mediator determines that an impasse has occurred.
    *   Either party desires to end the mediation.
7. The dispute management option offered by the UNM Mediation Clinic is one that facilitates communication effectiveness without aiming to place blame or find guilt.

8. Participation in mediation is voluntary and does not preclude the use of any other dispute resolution offices at the University of New Mexico.
9. Participants in the mediation process do not waive any rights to seek recourse using any other dispute resolution office at the University of New Mexico.

We agree to the above-mentioned terms for undertaking mediation:

_____

signature   date

_____

signature   date

Standards of Confidentiality

1. These sessions will be held in strict confidence by the mediators. Specifically, they will not voluntarily reveal any of the content of the session to any other person.

Exceptions to Strict Confidentiality:

a. Mediators will reveal to appropriate individuals those issues that are required by law to be revealed, namely, child abuse or physical danger to a person.

b. Mediators may consult with another person who shares the same standard of confidentiality; for instance, if a consultation is needed with another expert in communication, personnel, or legal issues, that person would be advised of this policy and would be bound to confidentiality.

c. It may be revealed to appropriate persons that the meetings were held, how often they were held, and that the process is completed.

d. Any information that all parties, including the mediators, agree may be revealed to others will be communicated after all have had time to review that information in writing.

e. Information will be collected from parties and mediators at the close of the process regarding resolution of issues and satisfaction with the process. This information will be presented in summary form by the UNM Mediation Clinic and

will not contain information allowing identification
of the parties.

2. The UNM Mediation Clinic will try to block any
    effort from any source that attempts to obtain
    information about the content of the sessions or
    the opinions of the mediators.

3. The clients are not bound by confidentiality, and
    are in fact encouraged to seek advice and
    consultation. Discretion is requested of them, but
    is not demanded.

4. No one besides the parties and the mediators will
    be involved in these meetings unless all agree that
    their presence is necessary. If all agree that any
    other person should join the sessions, that person
    would have to agree to the provisions of this
    statement prior to joining a session.

5. This document is an entire statement of the
    participants' agreement to work together and is
    not confidential. It has been prepared to ensure an
    environment that is conducive to open discussion,
    and will be relied upon in the future to document
    the shared understanding of privacy should that
    be required.

name_____date_____

COMMUNITY MEDIATION SERVICE
1221 PEACEFUL STREET
TOWN, STATE
PHONE

_____

The mediation session between
_____and_____

was held this_____ day of _____,

19_____ with

mediators_____and_____.

The parties have agreed to the following:

Signed this _____day of _____, 19_____

Parties
_____and_____

Mediators
_____and_____

Sample Mediation Introduction

Hello! Welcome to mediation at the Community Mediation Center. My name is Kathy Domenici, and this is Jeff Grant. We will be your mediators tonight and would like to take this opportunity to commend you on choosing this method to address your dispute. Would a first-name basis be OK tonight? Thanks Jim, Jane. Let's begin by defining the mediation process and let you know what you can expect here tonight.

Mediation is a dispute resolution process where mediators are impartial third parties who help you work out an understanding that is acceptable to both of you. We will help you explore the situation and recognize the issues that are conflicting you. We will begin by asking you both to explain the situation that has brought you here tonight. We will identify and agree on the basic issues and work together to explore them and generate options toward agreement. Our goal is to help you find a resolution with which you are both comfortable.

Our role here tonight as mediators is to serve as facilitators. We will not make decisions for you or give suggestions. We are not here as lawyers or judges or counselors, but as communication guides to discuss solutions for the future.

Anything you say here tonight will be confidential. You may see us taking notes and you are free to do so, too. These notes will be destroyed at the end of the session.

We follow some common courtesy guidelines. It is in everyone's best interests to keep our discussions civil and balanced. Everyone will have a chance to say what they need to. If you have something to say when someone else is speaking, jot it down on paper to be discussed later. In other words, no interrupting! Do either of you have any ground rules you feel would be necessary?

Sometimes mediations reach an impasse, and we call a caucus. This is a break in the process, where we will meet with each of you separately. Information given in a caucus may be kept confidential if you so desire. Do either of you have any questions?

We'd like to begin here by having each of you explain your perspective on the situation. Jane, you brought this case to the Mediation Center—why don't you begin?

Questions/Statements to Facilitate Movement

The following phrases help individuals give information on content and feelings, as they move toward resolution. These statements can be used in the storytelling stage, problem-solving stage, or agreement stage to clarify issues, elicit more information, and reality check possible options or solutions.

- Let me see if I've heard you correctly, you're saying . . .
- It sounds to me like you feel . . .
- Can you tell us some more about . . .
- What happened to lead up to this situation?
- Are there any other details that contributed to this problem?
- How did you feel?
- What do you need to feel better about this situation?
- What could _____ do to help this problem be resolved?
- What is it about _____ that makes you feel _____?
- Can you explain to us what you just heard _____ say?
- What will this mean to you?
- How will this affect your family/working/relationship?
- I hear you saying . . . is that correct?
- So you wish that . . .

Statements to STOP Movement

These phrases hinder individuals from exploring issues by revealing content and feelings. These statements imply judgements or advice on the mediator's part that takes control away from the parties. These statements also can reduce trust in the process as the parties feel the control being taken away from them. These statements could also evoke defensiveness, as parties feel like they have to justify their actions, statements.

- You ought to/you need to . . .
- Why didn't you do this . . . ?
- That doesn't seem like a very important issue.
- I suggest that you . . .
- That would be a bad choice for you.
- You are wrong about that.
- How could you feel that way—you know better than that!
- Everyone has those feelings.
- You can do better than that.
- Don't feel like that.
- Don't believe that way.

Cases for Use in Simulations/Role-Plays

Workplace Conflict

This is a case between the owner of a private advertising agency and the supervisor of the other five employees of the agency. There has been some underlying tension in the workplace—a small building with one main common area, an office for the owner, an office for the supervisor, and five cubicles for the artists. In the common area is a conference table, copy machine, fax machine, coffee and snack area, and reception area.

The owner, B. Smith, sixty years old, has built this business from scratch. In the increasingly competitive advertising community, this ad agency has struggled to remain in the top three advertising agencies in Albuquerque for the last ten years. The owner is hoping to bring in enough profit this year to open a Santa Fe office next year.

The owner has an authoritarian style of doing business, desiring efficiency without sacrificing quality. This owner hand-selected the supervisor and the five artists, leads the weekly staff meeting, sets the agenda and issues, and makes decisions. The banner over the owner's desk reads, "The man who rows the boat doesn't have time to rock it." The message coming from the owner is to keep the momentum but not to sacrifice any employees.

The supervisor, D. Jones, doesn't feel valued. Managing five professional artists and keeping them motivated and satisfied is an immense responsibility. The supervisor does not feel that he/she has a voice in the company. For example, the supervisor feels continually shut out at staff meetings. The supervisor wants to offer professional education and incentives such as going to conferences, workshops and trying new techniques. The supervisor feels that the success of major advertisers is the result of flexibility, the opportunity to "stretch." Three of the artists have a special interest in a new video technique using 3-D images, and the supervisor is interested in encouraging experimentation with a couple of the clients.

The supervisor and the owner saw their conflict brought to a head after the last staff meeting. The supervisor was incensed after the owner took credit for a slogan advertising a new juice drink. The supervisor remembers mentioning the idea for the slogan to the owner in a conversation that week. At the staff meeting, the owner presented it as his/her brainstorm. This led to a short, heated exchange of words at the meeting. Before they both left the office that day, they had words again and tempers rose further. The supervisor said the issue is much bigger than just credit for that one idea, it is a matter of respect where respect is due. The owner sticks to the issue of the credited idea, remembering clearly when it was hatched. The supervisor suggested mediators from the local neighborhood association to help them resolve the conflict. The owner agreed, not wanting to waste time arguing and affecting productivity.

Barking Dog

M. Jones has been complaining about the barking of his neighbor's dog. Jones attempted to bring the matter up with neighbor M. Brown, but has never been able to find Brown at home during the day. Jones contacted the Neighborhood Dispute Resolution office, which then called Brown and issued an invitation to mediation. Brown agreed.

Jones, a twenty-year resident of the neighborhood, has been increasingly bothered by the barking of the dog at night, particularly about 3 A.M. Jones and his wife are both retired and have trouble getting back to sleep once awakened. They are proud of their neighborhood activities and are active in the local association. Each year, Mr. and Mrs. Jones host the neighborhood picnic. They occasionally have their grandchildren over for the night, which is particularly troublesome when they are awakened. Jones feels very generous in not calling the police and using mediation instead.

Brown is a pilot with Fasttrack Airlines. He works odd hours and sleeps odd hours. Brown is a single person who moved into the neighborhood six months ago. Having a dog is an important security precaution for Brown, coming from a large city where there was a lot of crime. Brown has never before had complaints and thought the dog would be an asset to the neighborhood. Brown hopes to stay in the area for a long time and has just been too busy to meet the neighbors. Unfortunately, Brown is a stubborn person and a firm believer in personal rights, especially in one's own yard and home. The invitation to mediation was a surprise and an imposition on Brown's busy schedule.

Tenant-Landlord

Tenant rents a small bungalow in the far back end of Landlord's property. The parties have a verbal agreement that Tenant would rent for another year, but neither party is happy with the way things are going. Tenant pays $400 a month and was hoping to have a washer/dryer installed, as was discussed in a conversation six months ago. Landlord wants Tenant to share more in the yard responsibility and wants to increase the rent by $25 a month.

Tenant wants to continue to rent the apartment but is a student and cannot afford any additional cost. Tenant had believed that Landlord "promised" to put in the washer/dryer and thinks Landlord is putting that off so the rent can be raised. Tenant wants to continue to pay the $400 a month for the next year and is then willing to renegotiate the rent. Tenant wonders why Landlord is now going back on promises. Tenant enjoys the company of Landlord, and they previously would talk and share a cup of coffee.

Landlord wants to maximize potential profit from rental property. Similar rentals in the area go for at least $500 a month, and Landlord feels that this has been quite a generous arrangement. Landlord was recently divorced and is short of funds. Putting in a washer/dryer is an impossibility unless the rent could be raised. Landlord is also hesitant to give anything more to Tenant, since Landlord has been expecting some help with the yardwork and is not seeing any. Landlord feels overwhelmed with responsibility and sees that raising the rent to an appropriate amount and sharing some of the responsibilities could put them both on the right path.

To Smoke or Not to Smoke

Pat and Chris work in the same office of a large law firm. Pat smokes and Chris does not. The firm has a designated smoking area outside near the lobby doors, and Pat uses this area regularly. Chris is still bothered by the smoke smell on Pat's clothes and the coughing fits. Their desks are right next to each other, with a window on the wall at their backs. Both Pat and Chris do computer typing most of the day.

Pat enjoys being a smoker despite realizing the damage it does to the body. Pat continues to smoke at work during breaks and at lunch, using the designated smoking area. Pat resents Chris's complaints and is tempted to respond with a complaint about Chris's strong-smelling toiletries.

Chris dislikes the smell of smoke or tobacco and can smell it in the air in the office, on Pat's clothes, in Pat's hair, and on Pat's breath. Chris is annoyed and feels it is a violation of personal space to have to breathe stale smoke smell. Chris also has strong allergies, which make breathing difficult in the spring and summer.

In the following "tag-team" role-play, select two individuals (preferably from outside the class) to be the two disputants. Students will play the mediators in a co-mediation process. Each student should take a turn playing mediator for approximately ten minutes or until some substantial movement is seen or information gained. Turns at role-playing end when a "mediator" is tapped by the next student to role-play.

Saggy Pants

Mesa Vista High School is in a metropolitan area with a population of approximately 600,000. The school is one of ten high schools in the district and serves a racially and socioeconomically diverse neighborhood.

The initiating disputant, D. Wade, has been suspended twice by Mesa Vista High School for wearing "saggy pants"—loose fitting pants worn low on the hips, usually showing undergarments. Many gangs wear this type of attire to show their gang colors (on the undergarments). D. Wade has been advised by the school that returning to school wearing saggy pants will result in expulsion.

D. Wade claims that wearing saggy pants is an attempt to display solidarity with an urban minority culture. D. Wade feels that the school district's policy is an infringement on freedom of expression and a callous disregard for minority culture.

The principal of Mesa Vista, K. Johnson, defends the school's policy of dress codes on the grounds of protecting the educational environment and safety of the campus. The school district's legal counsel has advised the school district to attempt to mediate the dispute to avoid litigation.

Mediation Observation

With help from your instructor, locate an opportunity to observe a mediation (the Yellow Pages may provide places). While observing, the following questions can be addressed.

1) Where was the mediation observed? Briefly, what was the dispute about?
2) Did any issues arise during the course of the mediation other than the positions first given?
3) Did one disputant seem to have more power than the other? How did the mediators work at empowering each party?
4) Was an agreement reached? Do you think both parties were satisfied? Briefly describe.

Explore and comment on any of the following:

1) **Nonverbal communication**:
   Eye contact
       Each disputant with the mediators
       Disputants with each other
       Mediators with each other
   Physical environment—chairs, atmosphere, etc.
   Touching
   Physical space (proxemics)
   Time (chronemics)

2) **Stages of mediation**:
   Describe which of these stages were apparent and what happened in each.
       Introduction
       Story-telling stage

   Problem-solving stage
   Resolution stage

3) **Language:**
   Did you notice any words or sentences that helped
   create a safe environment?

   What emotional language was used? How did the
   mediators and/or disputants respond?

   Did you notice any language that seemed to place
   blame or find guilt? How did the other respond?

References

Adler, R. B. & Towne, N. (1990). *Looking Out Looking In: Interpersonal Communication*, 6th ed. Fort Worth, TX: Holt, Rinehart & Winston.

Bohannan, P. (1992). *We, The Alien: An Introduction to Cultural Anthropology.* Prospect Heights, IL: Waveland.

Bush, R. A. B. & Folger, J. P. (1994). *The Promise of Mediation: Responding to Conflict Through Empowerment and Recognition.* San Francisco: Jossey-Bass.

Carter, J. (1993). *Talking Peace: A Vision for the Next Generation.* New York: Penguin.

Crum, T. F. (1987). *The Magic of Conflict.* New York: Simon & Schuster.

Donohue, W. A. with Kolt, R. (1992). *Managing Interpersonal Conflict.* Newbury Park: Sage.

Fagre, L. (1995). "Recognizing Disputant's Face-needs in Community Mediation." Paper presented at Western States Communication Association Conference. Feb. 1995.

Fisher, R. & Ury, W. (1981). *Getting To Yes: Negotiating Agreement Without Giving In.* Boston: Houghton Mifflin.

Folger, J. P. & Poole, M. S. (1984). *Working through Conflict: A Communication Perspective.* Glenview, IL: Scott, Foresman.

Foss, S. K. & Foss, K. A. (1994). *Inviting Transformation: Presentational Speaking for a Changing World.* Prospect Heights, IL: Waveland.

Goffman, E. (1959). *The Presentation of Self in Everyday Life.* Garden City, NY: Doubleday.

Grant, J. Mediator, University of New Mexico Mediation Clinic, Albuquerque, NM.

Hocker, J., & Wilmot, W. (1991). *Interpersonal Conflict*, 3rd ed. Dubuque, IA: Wm. C. Brown.

Kaufman, G. & Raphael, L. (1983). *The Dynamics of Power: Building a Competent Self.* Rochester, VT: Schenkman Books.

121

Kolb, D. M. & Associates. (1994). *When Talk Works: Profiles of Mediators.* San Francisco: Jossey-Bass.

Lakoff, G. & Johnson, M. (1980). *Metaphors We Live By.* Chicago: University of Chicago Press.

Littlejohn, S., Shailor, J. & Pearce, W. B. (1994). "The Deep Structure of Reality in Mediation." In J. P. Folger & T. S. Jones (eds.), *New Directions in Mediation: Communication Research and Perspectives.* Newbury Park, CA: Sage.

Lulofs, R. S. (1994). *Conflict: From Theory to Action.* Scottsdale, AZ: Gorsuch Scarisbrick.

Moore, C. (1986). *The Mediation Process.* San Franciso: Jossey-Bass.

Olson, C. (1994). *Basic Meeting Facilitation Skills Training.* Cynthia Olson & Associates, P.O. Box 30026, Albuquerque, NM 97190-0026.

Pearce, W. B. & Littlejohn, S. W. (in press). *When Social Worlds Collide: The Management of Moral Conflict.* Thousand Oaks, CA: Sage.

Sunoo, J. J. (1990). "Some Rules of Thumb for Intercultural Mediators." *Negotiation Journal,* October 1990.

Williams, G. (1983). *Legal Negotiation and Settlement.* Minneapolis: West Publishing.

Wilson, S. R. & Putnam, L. L. (1990). "Interaction Goals in Negotiation." In James A. Anderson (ed.), *Communication Yearbook 13.* Newbury Park, CA: Sage.

Wolvin, A. & Coakley, C. G. (1988). *Listening,* 3rd ed. Dubuque, IA: W. C. Brown.

Verderber & Verderber (1992). *Inter-act: Using Interpersonal Communication Skills.* Belmar, CA: Wadwsorth.

Suggested Reading

Abel, R. L. (1982). *The Politics of Informal Justice*. New York: Academic Press.

Alger, C., & Stohl, M. (eds.) (1988). *A Just Peace Through Transformation: Cultural, Economic, and Political Foundations for Change*. Boulder, CO: Westview Press.

Allen, M., Donahue, W., & Stewart, B. (1990). Comparing Hardline and Softline Bargaining Strategies in Zero-Sum Situations Using Meta-Analysis. In M. A. Rahim (ed.), *Theory and Research in Conflict Management* (pp. 86–103). New York: Praeger.

Allison, G. T., Carnesale, A., & Nye, J. S., Jr. (eds.) (1985). *Hawks, Doves and Owls: An Agenda for Avoiding Nuclear War*. New York: W. W. Norton.

Allison, G. T., Ury, W. L., & Allyn, B. J. (1989). *Windows of Opportunity: From Cold War to Peaceful Competition in U.S.-Soviet Relations*. Cambridge, MA: Ballinger.

Antilla, Susan. (1995). The Next Magic Bullet? Mediation. *The New York Times*, 5 February.

Assefa, H. (1987). Mediation of Civil Wars. In *Approaches and Strategies—The Sudan Conflict*. Boulder, CO: Westview Press.

Auerbach, J. (1983). *Justice Without Law?* New York: Oxford University Press.

Axelrod, R. (1984). *The Evolution of Cooperation*. New York: Basic Books.

Bacharach, S. B. (1983). Bargaining within Organizations. In M. H. Bazerman & R. J. Lewicki (eds.), *Negotiating in Organizations* (pp. 360–76). Beverly Hills: Sage.

Bacharach, S. B., and Lawler, E. J. (1980). Power and Politics in Organizations.In *The Social Psychology of Conflict, Coalitions, and Bargaining*. San Francisco: Jossey-Bass.

———. (1981). *Bargaining: Power, Tactics and Outcomes*. San Francisco: Jossey-Bass.

———. (1986). Power Dependence and Power Paradoxes in Bargaining. *Negotiation Journal*, 2: 167–74.

Bacow, L. S., & Wheeler, M. (1984). *Environmental Dispute Resolution*, Chapter 8. New York: Plenum Press.

Bart, J., Beisecker, T., & Walker, G. (1989). Knowledge versus Ignorance as Bargaining Strategies: The Impact of Knowledge about Other's Information Level. *The Social Science Journal*, 26(2): 161–72.

Bartos, O. J. (1974). *Process and Outcome of Negotiations*. New York: Columbia University Press.

Bazerman, M. H., & Carroll, J. S. (1987). Negotiator Cognition. In L. L. Cummings & B. M. Staw (eds.), *Research in Organizational Behavior*, 9: 247–88. Greenwich, CT: JAI Press.

Bercovitch, Jacob. (1992). Mediators and Mediation Strategies in International Relations. *Negotiation Journal* (April).

Bernard, S. E., Folger, J. P., Weingarten, H. R., and Zumeta, Z. R. (1984). The Neutral Mediator: Value Dilemmas in Divorce Mediation. *Mediation Quarterly*, 4: 49-60.

Bies, R. J., Shapiro, D. L., & Cummings, L. L. (1988). Causal Accounts and Managing Organizational Conflict. *Communication Research Special Issue: Communication, Conflict and Dispute Resolution*, 15: 381–99.

Bigoness, W. J., & Kesner, I. F. (1986). Mediation Effectiveness: What Can We Learn from Leadership Research. In R. J. Lewicki, B. H. Sheppard, & M. H. Bazerman (eds.), *Research on Negotiations in Organization*, 1: 229–49.

Blake, R., & Mouton, J. S. (1984). *Solving Costly Organizational Conflicts*. San Francisco: Jossey-Bass.

Blalock, H. M., Jr. (1989). *Power and Conflict: Toward a General Theory*. Newbury Park, CA: Sage.

Boehringer, G. H., Zeruolis, V., Bayley, J., & Boehringer, K. (1974). Stirling: The Destructive Application of Group Techniques to a Conflict. *Journal of Conflict Resolution*, 18: 257–75.

Bowser, B. P., Auletta, G. S., & Jones, T. (1993). *Confronting Diversity Issues on Campus*. Newbury Park, CA: Sage.

Braiker, H. B., & Kelley, H. H. (1979). Conflict in the Development of Close Relationships. In R. L. Burgess & T. L. Huston (eds.), *Social Exchange in Developing Relationships* (pp. 135–68). New York: Academic Press.

Brand, N. (1992). Learning to Use the Mediation Process: A Guide for Lawyers. *Arbitration Journal* (December).

Brett, J. M., Drieghe, R., & Shapiro, D. L. (1986). Mediator Style and Mediation Effectiveness. *Negotiation Journal, 2:* 277–86.

Brookmire, D. A., & Sistrunk, F. (1980). The Effects of Perceived Ability and Impartiality of Mediators and Time Pressure on Negotiations. *Journal of Conflict Resolution, 24* (June): 311–27.

Brown, L. D. (1992). Normative Conflict Management Theories: Past, Present, and Future. *Journal of Organizational Behavior, 13:* 303–9.

Burrell, N. A., Donahue, W. A., & Allen, M. (1988). Gender-based Perceptual Bias in Mediation. *Communication Research Special Issue: Communication, Conflict and Dispute Resolution, 15:* 447–69.

———. (1990). The Impact of Disputants' Expectations on Mediation: Testing an Interventionist Model. *Human Communication Research, 17:* 104–39.

Bush, R. A., & Folger, J. P., (1994). *The Promise of Mediation: Responding to Conflict through Empowerment and Recognition.* San Francisco: Jossey-Bass.

Cahn, D. D. (1990). Intimates in Conflict: A Research Review. In D. D. Cahn (ed.), *Intimates in Conflict: A Communication Perspective* (pp. 1–24). Hillsdale, NJ: Lawrence Erlbaum.

Carnevale, P. J. D. (1986). Strategic choice in mediation. *Negotiation Journal, 2,* 41–56.

———. (1986). Mediating Disputes and Decisions in Organizations. In R. J. Lewicki, B. H. Sheppard, & M. H. Bazerman (eds.), *Research on Negotiations in Organization, 1:* 251–69.

Carnevale, P., & Pegnetter, R. (1985). The Selection of Mediation Tactics in Public Sector Disputes: A Contingency Analysis. *Journal of Social Issues, 41:* 65–81.

Cobb, S. (1994). A Narrative Perspective on Mediation: Toward the Materialization of the "Storytelling" Metaphor. Orientations to Conflict, and Mediation Discourse. In J. P. Folger & T. S. Jones (eds.), *New Directions in Mediation* (pp. 48–63). Thousand Oaks, CA: Sage.

Cohen, H. (1980). *You Can Negotiate Anything.* Secarus, NJ: Lyle Stuart.

Comstock, J., & Buller, D. B. (1991). Conflict Strategies Adolescents Use with Their Parents: Testing the Cognitive Communicator Characteristics Model. *Journal of Language and Social Psychology, 10*: 47–60.

Corcoran, K. O. and Melamed, J. C. (1989). From Coercion to Empowerment: Spousal Abuse and Mediation. *Mediation Quarterly, 7*: 303–16.

Costello, Edward J., Jr. (1992). The Mediation Alternative in Sex Harassment Cases. *Arbitration Journal* (March).

Courtright, J. A., Millar, F. E., Rogers, L. E., & Bagarozzi, D. (1990). Interaction Dynamics of Relational Negotiation: Reconciliation versus Termination of Distressed Relationships. *Western Journal of Speech Communication, 154*: 429–53.

Cue, W., & Walker, G. B. (1987). Advocacy and Influence in Integrative Negotiation: "Win-Win" Argumentation. In J. W. Wenzel (ed.), *Argument and Critical Practices: Proceedings of the Fifth SCA/AFA Conference on Argumentation*. Annandale, VA: Speech Communication Association.

Cushman, D. P., & King, S. S. (1985). National and Organizational Cultures in Conflict Resolution: Japan, the United States, and Yugoslavia. In W. B. Gudykunst, L. P. Stewart, & S. Ting-Toomey (eds.), *Communication, Culture, and Organizational Processes* (pp. 114–33). Beverly Hills: Sage.

Davidow, J. (1979). *A Peace in Southern Africa: The Lancaster House Conference on Rhodesia*. Boulder, CO: Westview Press.

Davis, A. M., & Salem, R. A. (1984). Dealing with Power Imbalances in the Mediation of Interpersonal Disputes. *Mediation Quarterly, 6*: 17–26.

De Waal, F. (1994). Conflict Resolution. In J. J. Bonsignore, E. Katsh, P. d'Errico, R. M. Pipkin, S. Arons, & J. Rifkin (eds.), *Before the Law: An Introduction to the Legal Process* (5th ed.) (pp. 485–86). Palo Alto, CA: Houghton Mifflin.

Deetz, S. (1990). Reclaiming the Subject Matter as a Guide to Mutual Understanding: Effectiveness and Ethics in Interpersonal Interaction. *Communication Quarterly, 38*: 226–43.

DeStephen, D. (1987). Mediating Power Imbalances: The Mediator's Responsibility to Protect Disputants from Unfair Solutions. Paper presented at the annual convention of the Speech Communication Association (November), Boston, MA.

Deutsch, M. (1973). *The Resolution of Conflict: Constructive and Destructive Processes*. New Haven, CT: Yale University Press.

Diez, M. E. (1986). Negotiation Competence: A Conceptualization of the Rules of Negotiation Interaction. In D. G. Ellis & W. A. Donohue (eds.), *Contemporary Issues in Language and Discourse Processes*. Hillsdale, NJ: Lawrence Erlbaum.

Donahue, W. A. (1981). Analyzing Negotiation Tactics: Development of a Negotiation Interact System. *Human Communication Research*, 7: 273–87.

———. (1989). Criteria for Developing Communication Theory in Mediation. In M. A. Rahim (ed.), *Managing Conflict* (pp. 71–82).

———. (1989). Communication Competence in Mediators. In K. Kressel & D. G. Pruitt (eds.), *Mediation Research: The Process and Effectiveness of Third-Party Intervention* (pp. 322–42). San Francisco: Jossey-Bass.

———. (1991). *Communication, Marital Dispute and Divorce Mediation*. Hillsdale, NJ: Lawrence Erlbaum.

Donahue, W. A., Allen, M., & Burrell, N. (1988). Mediator Communicative Competence. *Communication Monographs, L5*: 104–19.

Donohue, W. A., & Bresnahan, M. I. (1994). Communication Issues in Mediating Cultural Conflict. In J. P. Folger & T. S. Jones (eds.), *New Directions in Mediation* (pp. 135–58). Thousand Oaks, CA: Sage.

Donohue, W. A., Diez, M. E., & Hamilton, M. (1984). Coding Naturalistic Negotiation Interaction. *Human Communication Research*, 10: 403–25.

Donohue, W., & Kolt, R. (1994). *Managing Interpersonal Conflict*. Newbury Park, CA: Sage.

Donohue, W. A., Ramesh, C., Kaufmann, G., & Smith, R. (1991). Crisis bargaining in Intense Conflict Situations. *International Journal of Group Tendencies, 21*, 133–45.

Donohue, W. A. & Roberto, A. (1993). Relational Developments as Negotiated Order in Hostage Negotiation. *Human Communication Research, 20*(2): 175–98.

Druckman, D., Broome, B. J., & Korper, S. H. (1988). Value Differences and Conflict Resolution: Facilitation or Delinking? *Journal of Conflict Resolution, 32*(3): 489–510.

Elkouri, F., & Elkouri, E. A. (1985). *How Arbitration Works* (4th ed.). Washington, DC: Bureau of National Affairs.

Ellis, D. G., & Fisher, B. A. (1975). Phases of Conflict in Small Group Development: A Markov Analysis. *Human Communication Research*, 1: 195–212.

Emond, P. (ed.) (1989). *Commercial Dispute Resolution: Alternatives to Litigation.* Aurora, Ontario, Canada: Law Books.

Feuille, P. (1992). Why Does Grievance Mediation Resolve Grievances? *Negotiation Journal*, 8(2): 131–45.

Feuille, P., & Kolb, D. (1994). Waiting in the Wings: Mediation's Role in Grievance Resolution. *Negotiation Journal*, 10(3).

Fisher, G. (1980). *International Negotiation: A Cross-Cultural Perspective.* Chicago: Intercultural Press.

Fisher, R. J. (1969). *International Conflict for Beginners.* New York: Harper and Row.

————. (1972). *Dear Israelis, Dear Arabs: A Working Approach to Peace.* New York: Harper and Row.

————. (1978). *International Mediation: A Workshop Guide.* New York: International Peace Academy.

————. (1983). Negotiating Power. *American Behavioral Scientist*, 27.

————. (1983). Third Party Consultation as a Method of Intergroup Conflict Resolution. *Journal of Conflict Resolution*, 27(2): 301–34.

————. (1985). Beyond Yes. *Negotiation Journal*, 2: 67-70.

————. (1994). *Beyond Machiavelli: Tools for Coping with Conflict.* Cambridge, MA: Harvard University Press.

Fisher, R., & Ury, W. (1981). *Getting to Yes: Negotiation Agreement without Giving In.* New York: Penguin Books.

Folberg, J. P., & Taylor, A. (1993). *Mediation: A Comprehensive Guide to Resolving Conflicts without Litigation.* San Francisco: Jossey-Bass.

Folger, J. P., & Bush, R. A. B. (1994). Ideology, Orientations to Conflict, and Mediation Discourse. In J. P. Folger & T. S. Jones (eds.), *New Directions in Mediation* (pp. 3–25). Thousand Oaks, CA: Sage.

Folger, J. P., & Jones, T. S. (eds.) (1994). *New Directions in Mediation.* Thousand Oaks, CA: Sage.

Folger, R. (1986). Mediation, Arbitration, and the Psychology of Procedural Justice. In R. J. Lewicki, B. H. Sheppard, & M. H. Bazerman (eds.), *Research on Negotiations in Organization*, Vol. 1 (pp. 57–59).

Freeman, S. A., Littlejohn, S. W., & Pearce, W. B. (1992). Communication and Moral Conflict. *Western Journal of Communication*, 56(4): 311–29.

Fuller, A. A. (1994). Conflict Resolution: Bane or Boost to Peace and Justice? In J. J. Bonsignore, E. Katsh, P. d'Errico, R. M. Pipkin, S. Arons, & J. Rifkin (eds.), *Before the Law: An Introduction to the Legal Process* (5th ed.) (pp. 512–14). Palo Alto, CA: Houghton Mifflin.

Gadlin, H. (1991). Careful Maneuvers: Mediating Sexual Harrassment. *Negotiation Journal*, 7(2): 139–53.

Gilligan, C. (1982). *In A Different Voice: Psychological Theory and Women's Development*. Cambridge, MA: Harvard University Press.

Gold, L. (1985). Reflections on the Transition from Therapist to Mediator. In J. A. Lemmon (ed)., Legal and Family Perspectives in Divorce Mediation. *Mediation Quarterly*, 9.

Goldberg, S. B. (1989). Grievance Mediation: A Successful Alternative to Labor Arbitration. *Negotiation Journal*, 5(1): 9–15.

Goldberg, S. B., Green, E., & Sander, F. (1995). *Dispute Resolution*. Boston, MA: Little, Brown.

Hale, C. L., Bast, C., & Gordon, B. (1991). Communication within a Dispute Mediation: Interactant's Perceptions of the Process. *The International Journal of Conflict Mangement*, 2(2) (April): 139–58.

Hall, E. T. (1983). *Dance of Life*. New York: Anchor Books.

Helm, B. (1989). Mediators' Duties, Informed Consent and the Hatfields versus the McCoys. *Mediation Quarterly*, 21: 65–76.

Helm, B., & Scott, S. (1986). Advocacy in Mediation. *Mediation Quarterly*, 13: 69–76.

Hiltrop, J. M. (1989). Factors Associated with Successful Labor Mediation. In K. Kressel & D. Pruitt (eds.), *Mediation Research: The Process and Effectiveness of Third-party Intervention*. San Francisco: Jossey-Bass.

Himes, Joseph S. (1980). *Conflict and Conflict Management*. Athens: University of Georgia Press.

Ippolito, C. A., and Pruitt, D. G. (1990) Power Balancing in Mediation: Outcomes and Implications of Mediator Intervention. *The International Journal of Conflict Management,* 1: 341–56.

Jones, T. S. (1988). Phase Structures in Agreement and No-Agreement Mediation. *Communication Research Special Issue: Communication, Conflict and Dispute Resolution,* 15: 470–95.

Jones, T. S., & Brinkman, H. (1994). Teach Your Children Well: Recommendations for Peer Mediation Programs. In J. P. Folger & T. S. Jones, (eds.), *New Directions in Mediation* (pp. 159–74). Thousand Oaks, CA: Sage.

Kanitz, M. A. (1987). *Getting Apart Together: The Couple's Guide to a Fair Divorce or Separation.* San Luis Obispo, CA: Impact.

Karambayya, R., & Brett, J. M. (1994). Managerial Third Parties: Intervention Strategies, Process, and Consequences. In J. P. Folger & T. S. Jones (eds.), *New Directions in Mediation* (pp. 175–92). Thousand Oaks, CA: Sage.

Kelly, C. & Troester, R. (1991). *Peacemaking through Communication.* Annandale, VA: Speech Communication Association.

Kelman, H. C. (1994). Interactive Problem-solving: A Social-psychological Approach to Conflict Resolution. In J. J. Bonsignore, E. Katsh, P. d'Errico, R. M. Pipkin, S. Arons, & J. Rifkin (eds.), *Before the Law: An Introduction to the Legal Process* (5th ed.) (pp. 507–10). Palo Alto, CA: Houghton Mifflin.

Keltner, J. W. (1994). *The Management of Struggle: Elements of Dispute Resolution through Negotiation, Mediation and Arbitration.* Cresskill, NJ: Hampton Press.

King, W. C., Jr., & Miles, E. W. (1990). What We Know—And Don't Know—About Measuring Conflict: An Examination of the ROCI-11 and the OCCI Conflict Instruments. *Management Communication Quarterly,* 4: 222–43.

Klingel, S., & Martin, A. (eds.) (1988). *A Fighting Chance: New Strategies to Save Jobs and Reduce Costs.* Ithaca, NY: ILR Press.

Knapp, M. L., Putnam, L. L., & Davis, L. J. (1988). Measuring Interpersonal Conflict in Organizations: Where Do We Go from Here? *Management Communication Quarterly,* 1: 414–29.

Knebel, F., & Clay, G. S. (1987). *Before You Sue: How to Get Justice Without Going to Court.* New York: Morrow.

Kolb, D. M. (1983). *The Mediators*. Cambridge, MA: MIT Press.

————. (1983). Strategy and the tactics of mediation. *Human Relations, 36*: 247–68.

————. (1985). To be a mediator: Expressive tactics in mediation. *Journal of Social Issues, 41*, 11–26.

————. (1989). Labor Mediators, Managers, and Ombudsmen: Roles Mediators Play in Different Contexts. In K. Kressel & D. G. Pruitt (eds.), *Mediation Research: The Process and Effectiveness of Third-Party Intervention*. San Francisco: Jossey-Bass.

Kolb, D. M. & Assoc. (1994). *When Talk Works: Profiles of Mediators*. San Francisco: Jossey-Bass.

Kolb, D. M., & Glidden, P. A. (1986). Getting to Know Your Conflict Options. *Personnel Administrator, 31*: 77–89.

Kolb, D. M., & Putnam, L. L. (1992). The Multiple Faces of Conflict in Organizations. In R. J. Lewicki, B. H. Sheppard & M. H. Bazerman (eds.), *Research on Negotiations in Organization, 1*: 57–59.

Kolb, D. M., & Silbey, S. S. (1990). Enhancing the Capacity of Organizations to Deal with Disputes. *Negotiation Journal, 6*: 297–304.

Kraemer, K. D. (1992). Teaching Mediation: The Need to Overhaul Legal Education. *Arbitration Journal* (September).

Kramer, V. (1992). Mediation: Perils, Pitfalls and Benefits. *Mothering, 65*: 100–6.

Kressel, K. (1972). *Labor Mediation: An Exploratory Survey*. Albany, NY: Association of Labor Mediation Agencies.

————. (1985). *The Process of Divorce: How Professionals and Couples Negotiate Settlements*. New York: Basic Books.

Kressel, K., & Pruitt, D. (1989). *Mediation Research. The Process and Effectiveness of Third-Party Intervention*. San Francisco: Jossey-Bass.

Kritek, P. B. (1994). *Negotiating at an Uneven Table: Developing Moral Courage in Resolving Our Conflicts*. San Francisco: Jossey-Bass.

Lannamann, J. W. (1991). Interpersonal Communication Research as Ideological Practice. *Communication Theory, 1*: 179–203.

Lax, D. A., & Sebenius, J. K. (1985). The Power of Alternatives or the Limits of Negotiation. *Negotiation Journal, 1*: 163–80.

Lax, D. A., & Sebenius, J. K. (1986). *The Manager as Negotiator: Bargaining for Cooperation and Competitive Gain.* New York: The Free Press.

Leitch, M. L. (1987). The Politics of Compromise: A Feminist Perspective on Mediation. *Mediation Quarterly, 15*: 163–76.

Levine, M. I. (1986). Power Imbalances in Dispute Resolution. In E. Palenski & H. M. Launer (eds.), *Mediation: Contexts and Challenges* (pp. 63–76). Springfield, IL: Charles C. Thomas.

Lewicki, R. J., Weiss, S. E., & Lewin, D. (1992). Model of Conflict, Negotiation and Third-Party Intervention: A Review and Synthesis. *Journal of Organizational Behavior, 13*: 209–52.

Littlejohn, S. W., Shailor, J., & Pearce, W. G. (1994). The Deep Structure of Reality in Mediation. In J. P. Folger & T. S. Jones (eds.), *New Directions in Mediation* (pp. 67–83). Thousand Oaks, CA: Sage.

Lujan, D. (1994). The Quality of Justice. In J. J. Bonsignore, E. Katsh, P. d'Errico, R. M. Pipkin, S. Arons, & J. Rifkin (eds.), *Before the Law: An Introduction to the Legal Process* (5th ed.) (pp. 514–15). Palo Alto, CA: Houghton Mifflin.

Mayer, B. (1987). The Dynamics of Power in Mediation and Negotiation. *Mediation Quarterly, 16*: 75–86.

McEwen, C. A., & Maiman, R. J. (1989). Mediation in Small Claims Court: Consensual Processes and Outcomes. In K. Kressel & D. G. Pruitt (eds.), *Mediation Research: The Process and Effectiveness of Third-Party Intervention* (pp. 53–67). San Francisco: Jossey-Bass.

Merry, S. E. (1989). Mediation in Nonindustrial Societies. In K. Kressel & D. G. Pruitt (eds.), *Mediation Research: The Process and Effectiveness of Third-Party Intervention* (pp. 53–67). San Francisco: Jossey-Bass.

Moore, C. W. (1986). *The Mediation Process: Practical Strategies for Resolving Conflict.* San Francisco: Jossey-Bass.

———. (1994). Why Do We Mediate? In J. P. Folger & T. S. Jones (eds.), *New Directions in Mediation* (pp. 195–203). Thousand Oaks, CA: Sage.

Nierenberg, Gerard I. (1968). *The Art of Negotiation.* New York: Cornerstone Library Publications.

Peachey, D. E. (1989). What People Want from Mediation. In K. Kressel & D. G. Pruitt (eds.), *Mediation Research: The Process and Effectiveness of Third-Party Intervention* (pp. 300–21). San Francisco: Jossey-Bass.

Pruitt, D. G., McGillicuddy, N. B., Welton, G. L., & Fry, W. R. (1989). Process of Mediation in Dispute Settlement Centers. In K. Kressel & D. G. Pruitt (eds.), *Mediation Research: The Process and Effectiveness of Third-Party Intervention* (pp. 368–95). San Francisco: Jossey-Bass.

Pruitt, D. G., & Rubin, J. Z. (1986). Escalation and Stability. Chapter 5 in *Social Conflict*. NY: Random House.

Putnam, L. L. (1988). Communication and Interpersonal Conflict in Organizations. *Management Communication Quarterly*, 1: 293–301.

———. (1989). Negotiation and Organizing: Two Levels within the Weickian Model. *Communication Studies*, 40: 249–57.

———. (1990). Reframing Integrative and Distributive Bargaining: A Process Perspective. In B. H. Sheppard, M. H. Bazerman, & R. J. Lewicki (eds.), *Research on Negotiation in Organizations*, Vol. 2 (pp. 3–30). Greenwich, CT: JAI Press.

Putnam, L. L., & Folger, J. P. (1988). Communication, Conflict, and Dispute Resolution: The Study of Interaction and the Development of Conflict Theory. *Communication Research Special Issue: Communication, Conflict and Dispute Resolution*, 15: 349–60.

Rapoport, A., and Chammah, A. M. (1965). *Prisoner's Dilemma*. Ann Arbor: University of Michigan Press.

Rifkin, J. (1994). Mediation from a Feminist Perspective: Promise and Problems. In J. J. Bonsignore, E. Katsh, P. d'Errico, R. M. Pipkin, D. Arons, S., & J. Rifkin (eds.), *Before the Law: An Introduction to the Legal Process* (5th ed.) (pp. 498–501). Palo Alto, CA: Houghton Mifflin.

———. (1994). The Practitioner's Dilemma. In J. P. Folger & T. S. Jones (eds.), *New Directions in Mediation* (pp. 67–83). Thousand Oaks, CA: Sage.

Rifkin, J., & Katsh, E. (1994). Out of Court. In J. J. Bonsignore, E. Katsh, P. d'Errico, R. M. Pipkin, S. Arons, & J. Rifkin (eds.), *Before the Law: An Introduction to the Legal Process* (5th ed.) (pp. 495–98). Palo Alto, CA : Houghton Mifflin.

Rifkin, J., Millen, J., & Cobb, S. (1994). Toward a New Discourse for Mediation: A Critique of Neutrality. In J. J. Bonsignore, E. Katsh, P. d'Errico, R. M. Pipkin, S. Arons, & J. Rifkin (eds.), *Before the Law: An Introduction to the Legal Process* (5th ed.) (pp. 501–7). Palo Alto, CA: Houghton Mifflin.

Roehl, J., Royer, F., & Cook, R. (1989). Mediation in Interpersonal Disputes: Effectiveness and Limitations. In K. Kressel & D. G. Pruitt (eds.), *Mediation Research: The Process and Effectiveness of Third-Party Intervention* (pp. 44–68). San Francisco: Jossey-Bass.

Rogers, N., & McEwen, C. (1989). *Mediation: Law, Policy, Practice*. New York: The Lawyers Cooperative.

Rogers, N., & Salem, R. (1987). *A Student's Guide to Mediation and the Law*. New York: Matthew Bender.

Rothman, J. (1989). Supplementing Tradition: A Theoretical and Practical Typology for International Conflict Management. *Negotiation Journal, 5*: 265–78.

Rubin, J. Z., & Rubin, C. (1989). *When Families Fight*. New York: William Morrow.

Rubinstein, R. A., & Foster, M. (eds.) (1988). *The Social Dynamics of Peace and Conflict: Culture in International Society*. Boulder, CO: Westview Press.

Schaap, C., Buunk, B., & Kerkstra, A. (1988). Marital Conflict Resolution. In P. Noller & M. A. Fitzpatrick (eds.), *Perspectives on Marital Interaction* (pp. 203–44). Philadelphia: Multilingual Matters.

Schlueter, D. W. , Barge, J. K., & Blankenship, D. (1990). A Comparative Analysis of Influence Strategies Used by Upper and Lower-Level Male and Female Managers. *Western Journal of Speech Communication, 54*(1): 42–65.

Shailor, J. G. (1994). *Empowerment in Dispute Mediation: A Critical Analysis of Communication*. Westport, CT: Praeger.

Shaw, Margaret (1994). Courts Point Justice In a New Direction. *The National Law Journal, 4*: 11-94.

Sheppard, B. H. (1984). Third-Party Conflict Intervention: A Procedural Framework. In B. M. Staw & L. L. Cummings (eds.), *Research in Organizational Behavior, 6*: 141–90.

Sheppard, B. H. (1992). Conflict Research as Schizophrenia: The Many Faces of Organizational Conflict. *Journal of Organizational Behavior, 13*: 325–33.

Skratek, Sylvia. (1990). Grievance Mediation: Does It Really Work? *Negotiation Journal*, 6(3).

Stahler, G., DuCette, J., & Povich, E. (1990). Using Mediation to Prevent Child Maltreatment: An Exploratory Study. *Family Relations*, *39*: 317–22.

Stamato, Linda. (1992). Sexual Harassment in the Workplace: Is Mediation an Appropriate Forum? *Mediation Quarterly*, *10*(2).

Susskind, L. (1985). Mediating Public Disputes: A Response to the Skeptics. *Negotiation Journal*, 1(2).

Susskind, L., & Cruikshank, J. (1987). *Breaking The Impasse: Consensual Approaches to Resolving Public Disputes*. New York: Basic Books.

Thomas, K. (1992). Conflict and Conflict Management: Reflections and Update. *Journal of Organizational Behavior*, *13*: 265–74.

Ting-Toomey, S. (1988). Intercultural Conflict Styles: A Face-Negotiation Theory. In Y. Y. Kim & W. B. Gudykunst (eds.), *Theories in Intercultural Communication* (pp. 213–38). Beverly Hills: Sage.

Ting-Toomey, S., Gao, G., Trubisky, P., Yang, Z., Kim, H. S., Ling, S-L., & Nishida, T. (1991). Culture, Face Maintenance, and Styles of Handling Interpersonal Conflict: A Study of Five Cultures. *International Journal of Conflict Management*, *2*: 275–96.

Tracy, K., & Spradlin, A. (1994). Talking Like a Mediator: Conversational Moves of Experienced Divorce Mediators. In J. P. Folger & T. S. Jones (eds.), *New Directions in Mediation* (pp. 110–32). Thousand Oaks, CA: Sage.

Ury, W. L., Brett, J. M., and Goldberg, S. (1988). *Getting Disputes Resolved*. San Francisco: Jossey-Bass.

———. (1993). *Getting Disputes Resolved: Designing Systems to Cut the Costs of Conflict*. Cambridge, MA: Harvard Law School.

Vayrynen, R. (1991). To Settle or to Transform? Perspectives on the Resolution of National and International Conflicts. In R. Vayrynen (ed.), *New Directions in Conflict Theory* (pp. 1–25). Newbury Park: Sage.

Vidmar, N. (1986). The Mediation of Small Claims Court Disputes. In R. J. Lewicki, B. H. Sheppard, & M. H. Bazerman (eds.), *Research on Negotiations in Organization*, *1*: 187–208.

Walker, G. B. (1990). Cultural Orientations of Argument in International Disputes: Negotiating the Law of the Sea. In F. Korzenny & S. Ting-Toomey (eds.), *Communicating for Peace* (pp. 96–117). Newbury Park: Sage.

Wall, J. A., Jr., & Rude, D. E. (1989). Judicial Mediation of Settlement Negotiations. In K. Kressel & D. G. Pruitt (eds.), *Mediation Research: The Process and Effectiveness of Third-Party Intervention* (pp. 190–212). San Francisco: Jossey-Bass.

Weber, A. L., Harvey, J. H., & Orbuch, T. L. (1992). What Went Wrong: Communicating Accounts of Relationship Conflict. In M. L. McLaughlin, M. J. Cody, & S. J. Read (eds.), *Explaining One's Self to Others: Reason-Giving in a Social Context* (pp. 261–80). Hillsdale, NJ: Lawrence Erlbaum.

Welton, G. L., Pruitt, D. G., & McGillicuddy, N. B. (1988). The Role of Caucusing in Community Mediation. *Journal of Conflict Resolution*, 32(1), 181–202.

Westin, A. F., & Feliu, A. G. (1988). *Resolving Employment Disputes without Litigation*. Washington, DC: BNA Books.

Whelan, J. G. (1990). *The Moscow Summit, 1988: Reagan and Gorbachev in Negotiation*. Boulder, CO: Westview Press.

White, R. K. (1984). *Fearful Warriors: A Psychological Profile of U.S.-Soviet Relations*. New York: The Free Press.

Wilkins, A. L. (1989). *Developing Corporate Character: How to Successfully Change an Organization Without Destroying It*. San Francisco: Jossey-Bass.

Wilkinson, J. H. (ed.) (1990). *Donovan Leisure Newton and Irvine ADR Practice Book*. Colorado Springs: Wiley Law Publications.

Williams, Gerald. (1983). *Legal Negotiation and Settlement*. St. Paul, MN: West.

Wilson, S. R., & Waltman, M. S. (1988). Assessing the Putnam-Wilson Organizational Communication Conflict Instrument (OCCI). *Management Communication Quarterly*, 1: 367–88.

Womack, D. F. (1988). A Review of Conflict Instruments in Organizational Settings. *Management Communication Quarterly*, 1: 437–45.

Wondolleck, J. M. (1988). *Public Lands Conflict and Resolution: Managing National Forest Disputes*. New York: Plenum Press.

Woodhouse, T. (1988). *The International Peace Directory*. Plymouth, UK: Northcote House Publishers.

Yale, Diane. (1988). Metaphors in Mediating. *Mediation Quarterly*, 22 (Winter): 15–24.

Young, O. (1972). Intermediaries: Additional Thought on Third Parties. *Journal of Conflict Resolution*, 16: 1.

Zartman, I. William, & Berman, Marjorie. (1982). *The Practical Negotiator*. New Haven, CT: Yale University Press.